TALES FROM
THE CHAIR

THE HURT, THE HAUNTED, THE HEALED
AND EVERYTHING IN BETWEEN

VOLUME ONE

J. ALEXANDER

Published By

OWL ®
PUBLISHERS

www.owlpublishers.com

360 S Market St, San Jose, CA 95113,
United States.

Printed in the United States of America

DISCLAIMER

This book draws on my clinical experience and weaves composite stories inspired by transformative moments. All identifying details names, ages, histories, and circumstances—have been changed or generalized to protect privacy and comply with HIPAA and CMIA. These are not literal accounts, but reflections of the shared journey in therapy, honoring the courage of those who attend.

MESSAGE TO THE READERS

The stories you will read here come from the heart of my therapeutic work. While the individuals themselves remain private and protected, what shines through are the emotions, challenges, and triumphs that define the human journey of healing.

If you're a therapist, you already know that this work changes you—not all at once, but slowly, session by session, story by story. You may start out believing you're here to help others find themselves, only to realize somewhere along the way that they're helping you find yourself, too. These pages are for you. For the long nights when doubt whispers louder than purpose. For the moments you wonder if the work matters. I hope these stories remind you why you sat in the chair in the first place: to bear witness to the quiet, stubborn miracle of healing. To remember that empathy is strength, not fragility. And that showing up, even when the light flickers, is its own form of grace.

And if you're not a therapist—if you've wondered what it's like on the other side of the conversation—these stories are for you as well. They pull back the curtain on a world that often stays hidden: the human mess behind the professional calm, the moments that break us open, and the sacred hope that keeps us returning to the room. Maybe you'll see pieces of yourself in the people I write about. Perhaps you'll understand a little more about what it means to be heard—or to listen deeply. Healing is not reserved for those with degrees on their walls. It's something we're all reaching for, one truth at a time.

Whoever you are, if these stories have found their way to you, I don't believe it's by accident. I hope they speak to a part of you that has been quietly waiting to be heard.

DEDICATION

To my wife, whose love, patience, and faith in me made every long night possible. Your encouragement has been my anchor, and I could not have walked this path without you.

TABLE OF CONTENTS

CHAPTER 1 - A TALE OF BILL AND MARLA

It's not about the Cozy Home

"Criticism often comes disguised as concern, defensiveness as self-protection, contempt as humor, and stonewalling as calm detachment."

"When two people begin to hear each other not just with their ears, but with their hearts, it can feel like magic."

A TALE OF BILL AND MARLA

It's not about the Cozy Home

Couples therapy is one of the most challenging and emotionally charged forms of work I do. Some mornings, even before clients arrive, my office feels like a battlefield—its silence thick with the promise of conflict. The hum of the fluorescent lights presses down, and the faint scent of coffee lingers like the ghosts of past clients returning to haunt the room. It's as if the walls have recorded every conversation and argument ever spoken, and they themselves are holding onto resentment.

Before clients arrive, I try to soften the battlefield and thin the heavy energy that remains. I turn off the fluorescent lights, letting the directional lamps cast warmer pools of light across the room, leaving only the faintest trace of sunshine filtering through the blinds. I angle the chairs slightly toward each other—close enough to suggest connection but not confrontation. I take a slow, grounding breath and let it settle. Sometimes I light a candle or switch on a small lamp to soften the sterile edge of the space. These small gestures signal that this room is not a place for combat, but a place where hearing, seeing, and being seen might still be possible.

Nevertheless, in the heat of battle, words sharpen into weapons, silence becomes armor, and everyone swears the other person fired the first shot. It's a battle fought in the murky trenches of emotion—a war waged not with weapons, but with tense silences, clipped words, icy stares, and uncomfortable pauses. On those days, I feel less like a therapist and more like a soldier dropped into the middle of a fight, armed with nothing but a chair and a notepad, and guarded by the hope that both sides will survive long enough to hear each other.

And yet, if you asked me to name the work that feels the most rewarding, I wouldn't hesitate. This is it.

When a couple finds their way to my office, they're not just bringing each other. They're bringing everything—history, hurt, and their version of the truth—laid out like evidence in an invisible trial. Their emotions have become the victim, and therapy becomes the courtroom. Sometimes one partner hopes I'll play referee; sometimes both want me to be judge and jury. They want that moment where I lean back, fold my arms, and say, see? Your partner is wrong. You were right all along.

But that moment never comes. Not in my office.

In my sessions, couples are taught that the relationship itself is the patient. It's a living entity—delicate, complex, and constantly shifting. Treating it means noticing its breathing, its tension, its subtle movements. It's not about deciding who's more right or more wounded; it's about pulling both partners onto the same side of the table and pointing to the real problem: this fragile, living thing they built together is now struggling to breathe.

The work is delicate. Some problems are obvious, staring you in the face and testing every ounce of your clinical judgment; others lurk in the shadows— hidden, elusive, quietly beckoning your attunement. It demands empathy, curiosity, and the willingness to sit in the fog until the blurred issues inside come into focus. It requires therapeutic objectivity, the boldness to confront distorted thought, and the patience to steer clients toward understanding without pushing them. But when it clicks—when two people begin to hear each other not just with their ears but with their hearts, and when they fight together rather than against each other—it can feel like magic. That magic isn't rare, though it arrives gently, like the first shared breath after a storm. I've held space for couples who come with maps drawn from old wounds, only to redraw them side by side.

That's what I was hoping for, Bill and Marla.

They couldn't have come from more different worlds. Marla, in her late thirties or early forties, bore the marks of a hard-fought life—faint scars from old choices and a wary gaze shaped by past struggles. She had battled personal demons, including substance use, and whether by grit or grace, she emerged stronger through recovery programs and support networks. Beneath the rigid shell was a woman hungry for connection, a flicker of vulnerability hidden behind the armor.

Bill, about nine years older than Marla, had experienced a different kind of survival. He had spent two decades in a long-term partnership—raising children and building a home that looked steady from the outside, yet left him unsure of who he was when the house fell silent. The divorce carved a void he didn't quite know how to fill. His hands, though rugged from work, were neat and manicured, his posture precise—but a subtle stiffness remained, a tension that spoke to years of compromise and self-erasure.

They met the way more people meet than they care to admit—through an online message. It started light: photos of shared hobbies, jokes, small talk. Somewhere in those exchanges, they built a bridge strong enough to carry them to a date. In session, they recalled sending messages late at night—small flashes of humor and warmth that hinted at curiosity, maybe even hope. Their words carried the nervous excitement of two people stepping into the unknown together.

When they finally met, sparks flew. They found common ground in their love of restoring old treasures—the gleam of polished surfaces, hints of patina, the faint scent of aged wood and oil. For a while, it was enough. Until it wasn't. For Marla, those pursuits carried echoes of riskier times, while Bill was just beginning to find new purpose in them. From her own convictions, Marla wanted to step back; Bill wanted to lean in. On quieter evenings, they lingered over mismatched mugs of tea, trading stories of half-remembered travels and forgotten recipes from childhoods worlds apart—small anchors that held them until the undercurrents stirred.

They were still very much in love when they came to me. They said so—openly and sincerely. In fact, each told me this was the healthiest relationship they'd ever had. But something had shifted. They couldn't name it, only feel it—a vague tension that pulled at their interactions.

In our early sessions, I asked them to share their beginnings. They spoke fondly of nights curled up on a couch, talking until their eyes grew heavy. Back then, words flowed like water—unfiltered and unafraid. They weren't just hearing each other; they were seeing each other. In those moments, silence felt safe, and laughter came easily. Neither of them realized how fragile that kind of connection could be once their pasts began to creep in.

The question hung in the room: So, what happened?

We began working through the common pitfalls of relationships, using John Gottman's framework—specifically his "Four Horsemen of the Relationship Apocalypse" and their antidotes. Much of our work centered on learning to see, not just each other, but themselves, in the moments when conflict took over. I tried to help them recognize the subtle arrival of the Horsemen—criticism, defensiveness, contempt, and stonewalling—as they appeared in real time. Criticism often came disguised as concern, defensiveness as self-protection, contempt as humor, and stonewalling as calm detachment. The challenge was to catch these patterns before they gained momentum—to notice the shift in tone or body language that signaled a retreat from connection. Seeing was the first step; only then could they begin to choose a different response.

In one pivotal session, the crack in their connection revealed itself. Marla arrived tense. Her words were short, clipped at the edges. Static ran through her body like electricity. When I asked what was happening, she told me about a vivid nightmare—one that made her fear she was slipping back into old patterns. It rattled her, set the tone for the day, and by evening, all she wanted was to be at Bill's. She confessed she'd been hoping he would help steady her through the spiral.

I paused her there. Over the years, I've learned to listen for these moments—the subtle handoff of emotional responsibility. We explored it gently. Bill wasn't responsible for her mood, and it wasn't fair to place that weight on his shoulders.

He shared his side of the story. He had been set off by a tough day at work—irritable, depleted, not in the space to be anyone's anchor. What confused him was how quickly Marla shut down without telling him why. In that silence, his mind began to invent its own explanations, leading him to assume the worst about the relationship. He explained that Marla's shutting down often left him frightened that the relationship was over.

Marla agreed to try not to make Bill responsible for her emotions, but it was clear she didn't yet know how to take full ownership of them. I knew this would remain a point of contention for many sessions to come—until she could not only understand the concept but embody it. Still, I was optimistic that Bill would have the patience to endure the learning curve and not lose faith as Marla worked to grow.

Then, in a shift I didn't expect, Marla began talking about her dream—not the troubling nightmare, but *the dream.*

A vision of stability. The cozy home. A sense of roots. A little companion. Weekend getaways. Her voice softened, almost childlike. As she spoke, I found myself leaning in—not because of the words themselves, but because of how she was saying them, like someone peering through a window at a life they'd never had. She was lost in her imagination. Her words echoed countless others I've heard in this chair—partners voicing dreams of home and escape, each revealing the hidden fears beneath their longing.

While Marla painted her picture, I caught it—Bill's face told his story. First, a subtle grimace, then a clenched jaw, and finally, his body stiffening. He tried to hide by sinking lower into his chair, but the crossing of his arms was a dead giveaway. His attention drifted, his eyes fixing on a point far away. Anger, fear. I could see both long before he could name them. I wondered if he'd be able to. Would he use the "I" statements we'd been exploring? I knew that was wishful thinking. His posture suggested he was gearing up for battle.

When Marla paused, I turned to Bill.

"Bill," I said, "I see something's happening for you right now."

I didn't name the feelings. Calling them out too soon would have been like revealing the ending of an epic movie. Still, I wanted to see if he would apply the skills we'd practiced. As expected, he didn't. His passive-aggressive posture shifted into an attempt to express his feelings—an attempt that fell short.

He took a breath, then his words tumbled out, sharp and fast. "I've been there. I've done that. The home, the routines, the companion. The getaways. All of it."

Marla's face snapped out of her fantasy with visible shock. Her eyes widened, her mouth parted, as if the air had been sucked from the room. "So… you wouldn't want to do those things again?" she shot back, her tone unmistakably judgmental.

And there it was—an argument forming in the space between them. The air grew dense, charged with unspoken history. Bill leaned forward, his shoulders squared, eyes narrowing as if bracing for impact. Marla straightened in her chair, arms crossed tightly across her chest like armor. Their breathing shifted—his quick and shallow, hers held and deliberate. They spoke in overlapping half-sentences, not to connect but to defend. Criticism and defensiveness danced between them like practiced partners, each move predictable, each counterstrike rehearsed. Beneath it all, I could feel the same unspoken fear in both of them—the fear of being unseen, unheard, or worse, proven right about the other's worst assumption.

I let the argument run for a moment—just long enough to be certain of their misunderstanding. Then I intervened. Leaning forward, I raised my hand to shoulder height, fingers gently wiggling to draw their attention. "May I join your conversation?" I asked. They both nodded. I lowered my hand and settled back into my chair, saying nothing. I wanted to see if they would mirror my calm, to notice whether their posture would soften before I spoke again. It took a minute or two, but they did. Both sat back, their shoulders relaxed, their breathing slowed, and their arms unfolded. That was my invitation to speak.

"It's not about the cozy home," I said.

They both looked at me, puzzled. I held the space, letting the silence do its work and allowing the tension to settle. I've learned that silence often carries more weight than words—that waiting, resisting the urge to fill the void with unnecessary clatter, can make whatever comes next land with far greater meaning. It's a bit like a game of emotional chess—whoever moves first risks losing their position.

"What do you mean? It's not about the cozy home?" Marla asked.

I leaned forward slightly, resting my forearms on my knees. "I believe you're trying to communicate something on a much deeper level. Let's explore. What does it represent to you? The home. The roots. The companion. The getaways. What's underneath it?"

Marla was the first to speak. "It's something I've never had. A life I've never lived." Her words faltered, as if the sentence itself were heavy with longing. I sat up slightly, offering an empathic bridge. "Maybe it's less about the things themselves and more about what they represent—safety... comfort... security... connection... freedom?

She looked at me, her eyes lighting with recognition. "Exactly." I nodded.

Bill didn't hesitate. His voice was steady, clear. "To me, it's a prison."

He spoke of his previous relationship—the routines, expectations, the perfect family image—and how it had all been built within a controlling, suffocating structure. He hadn't been living; he had been performing. Every smile, every gesture, every act of love had been rehearsed under the weight of someone else's expectations. His legs had been cut out from under him, his sense of self buried beneath the constant need to keep the peace.

"It was the performance of a lifetime," he said quietly. "I'd work all day to provide, come home exhausted, only to face endless critiques about my efforts, my choices—feeling like I was always falling short." He described feeling trapped in his own life, like an actor locked onstage long after the audience had gone home—the weight of unspoken demands pressing down day after day, until the script no longer fit.

Marla turned toward Bill, and in a glance, understanding passed between them. Her prison had been forged in the guarded walls of raw survival and isolation. His had been shaped by polished routines, unspoken scripts, and steady facades. Their stories had seemed worlds apart—until this moment revealed the shared ache beneath them, the way both confinements whispered the same quiet plea for release.

Bill exhaled, the tension in his shoulders softening just slightly. "I just don't ever want to feel like that again," he said, his voice rough with exhaustion. "It's like I'm living someone else's idea of who I'm supposed to be."

Marla nodded, her eyes fixed on him. "I don't want to control you or make you return to your performance," she said quietly. "I just get scared when things start to feel out of control. I shut down before I even know what I'm doing. And once I shut down, I don't know how to start back up again." Marla paused, absorbing the honesty of her own words.

Bill spoke softly. "And I do want to offer safety, comfort, security, companionship… and be part of your freedom. I'm just not sure I know how."

Their words hung there—raw, unpolished, and authentic. They weren't defending their wounds; they were revealing them. And in that moment, I could see something new forming between them—something genuine enough to build on. Intrigued, they both turned toward me, curiosity sparking in their eyes. "How?" Bill asked. He didn't need to say anything more. I knew exactly what he was asking.

I told them about a skill I've learned over the years. "It's called listening with the third ear," I said. "It's a term coined by Theodor Reik, a psychoanalyst who spoke about going beyond hearing words—really tuning in to the emotions, the pauses, the unspoken messages beneath the surface," I explained that, over time, I've brought this into my daily life, not just therapy sessions. It's about noticing subtle cues, staying present, and allowing myself to be fully attentive without jumping to judgment or rushing to respond.

Using this skill has made me a better therapist—and a better person. It helps me stay grounded in my own emotions, even when my clients' experiences are intense or triggering. By listening with curiosity instead of assumption, I've been able to meet people where they are, understand the patterns beneath their words, and resist the urge to impose my own narrative. Listening beyond the words isn't just about what someone is saying—it's about creating space where insight can emerge for both of us. It has taught me patience, empathy, and the profound value of being fully present, even in silence—those serene intervals where the heart's true rhythm rises, unhurried and unseen.

Bill leaned forward and asked cautiously, "Is that… something we can learn?" His voice was tentative. Marla nodded, a hint of hope glowing in her eyes. "Can we really do that?" she added.

I smiled at them, leaning back slightly in my chair. "Absolutely," I said. "Like any skill, it takes practice and patience. It starts with small steps—learning to notice your own reactions first, to stay present, and to observe without judgment. Over time, you train yourself to catch not just the words someone says, but the emotions beneath them, the pauses, the tension, the little things that carry so much meaning—the flicker in a glance, the weight in a sigh, the space between breaths that holds a lifetime of untold stories."

I continued, "You'll stumble. You'll get frustrated. But every time you pause and really notice, you're strengthening the skill. It's not magic; it's intentional practice. And the more you do it, the more natural it becomes—in your relationship and in your own life—tightening that invisible scaffolding thread by thread until it holds against the storms."

We ended that session on a high note. Not all sessions end that way. Sometimes we leave feeling stalled, or worse, with the tension even heavier in the room. But this time was different. I asked them to practice listening with the third ear in the coming week—truly noticing each other's words, tone, and body language without interrupting or judging. To pause before responding, to reflect on what they were really hearing, and to speak from curiosity rather than assumption. The goal wasn't perfection; it was awareness, patience, and the willingness to show up differently, one small interaction at a time.

After they left, I sank back in my chair and let myself breathe, registering the subtle shifts that had taken place. I thought about the delicate architecture of relationships—the invisible scaffolding that holds people together through pain, hope, fear, and love—those unseen beams forged in quiet admissions and shared silences that echo long after words fade. There is no formula, no perfect script.

The work is as much about presence as it is about intervention. It requires the skill of observing and clearly naming whatever is in the room—emotions, energy, body language, unspoken truths—gently and without judgment or hurry. Each session reminds me that relationships can be chaotic yet resilient, and that change, however small, becomes possible when we are patient.

Bill and Marla still have a long road ahead—skills to build, habits to unlearn, and trust to repair. Yet they have begun the real work. In my chair, that's where change always starts: a slow, attentive dance that honors both who they are and who they might become. I look forward to walking this path with them, witnessing the beautiful process of transformation. Together, we are at the threshold of something new, something different, something more substantial—something built not on perfection but on presence, patience, and the courage to show up. And in thresholds like theirs, I've watched many begin their unraveling—not as an ending, but as an invitation to the life they've always circled, one unguarded step at a time.

CHAPTER 2 - A TALE OF ELENA

The Process of Healing

"Trauma isn't just a memory; it's a survival pattern etched into the body."

"Progress isn't linear. It lives in small, almost invisible increments—tiny bridges over chaos."

A TALE OF ELENA

The Process of Healing

For better or worse, the years I spent working in a residential treatment center are unforgettable. I can still feel the buzz of the fluorescent lights overhead, hear the shuffle of shoes on the linoleum, and the low murmur of voices drifting through the hallways. It was my fifth year as an addiction counselor, and I was transitioning into a clinical supervisor role while simultaneously pursuing a master's in counseling psychology—a painstaking juggling act that often left me running on coffee, notes, and sheer willpower. Before that, I had held nearly every position treatment centers offered.

Early in my career, I served as a case manager for two years, which led to a two-year stint as a residential treatment counselor. I was then offered a position as an Intensive Outpatient Counselor, followed by a promotion to IOP Coordinator. I was honored when the residential treatment program that gave me my start entrusted me with the opportunity to lead their clinical staff.

The years leading up to clinical supervision taught me the delicate balance of care, authority, and emotional endurance. I knew the role would involve less direct counseling and more management—supporting staff, guiding interns, and ensuring clients remained safe, engaged, and accounted for. Some days, the weight of responsibility pressed down so heavily that I could feel it in my chest. But I had experience, a CADC III credential, and a kind of stamina only forged by walking through chaos and emerging intact.

I wasn't new to demanding clients. I'd faced the aggressive, the rude, the confrontational, even the physically violent. I'd seen fists fly, doors slam, and words cut sharper than knives. The air in a residential program can shift in an instant—calm one moment, electric the next. As intense as they could feel, those moments were usually like ripples from a stone dropped into a lake—an initial shock that almost always faded fast. But then there was one client who, I realized almost immediately, would test the limits of everyone in the building— a woman whose anger rose and broke like storm waves, sudden and unpredictable swells capable of overwhelming a person in seconds.

From the moment she stepped through the door, her presence was magnetic and unsettling. She was impeccably dressed—head-to-toe polished, wrapped in name-brand clothing that whispered wealth and refinement. One might even call her posh. Yet the elegance ended at the surface. Beneath it was something wild, untamed, and sharp-edged—a feral energy at odds with her carefully curated appearance.

At first, it was an internal hypothesis; soon it became an undeniable truth. I knew she would make staff hold their breath, disrupt routines, and destabilize group dynamics. She would push boundaries, expose weaknesses, and test the very structure of our daily flow. Nothing about this client was going to be simple. Every day with her would demand everything from me and my counselors. I feared her presence would follow staff home at night, echoing in their thoughts long after their shifts ended. She had a gravity that bent everything around her.

We'll call her Elena.

Elena had been transferred from another residential program after repeated incidents: physical aggression, emotional outbursts, and calculated manipulation of both peers and staff. She sometimes isolated completely, refusing therapy or groups, only to swing hours later into intense emotional demands or explosive confrontation. Her moods were a storm without warning, and her fear of abandonment charged every interaction.

From the moment she arrived, the patterns we'd been warned about resurfaced. She swung between affection and fury, connection and withdrawal. One moment, she offered charm and compliments; the next, she accused others of betrayal or neglect. Her instability drained staff energy and unsettled clients, creating a tension that rippled through the building and left the entire environment on edge.

Complaints about Elena flooded my office daily—sometimes hourly. I felt as if I was drowning in the wake of her chaos. Staff and clients alike were pushed beyond their window of tolerance; everyone was functioning out of reaction, doing the best they could. Discharge felt inevitable. Nothing seemed to reach her. Every attempt at structure, every intervention, every therapy session felt like trying to hold back a tidal wave with one hand.

Inside, I was torn. One part of me sensed a person screaming for help—raw, desperate, terrified. Another part feared there was nothing left to salvage, that the chaos would never settle. I knew I had to hold both realities at once. I reminded myself of the principle Mr. Spock offered in *Star Trek*: *the needs of the many outweigh the needs of the few—or the one.* The safety of the program, the staff, and the other clients had to come first. We had tried. And it was beginning to look like we had failed.

Then the day came. After endless clinical discussions, consultations, and countless interventions, the moment we had all anticipated—and quietly dreaded—arrived. It was time to discharge Elena. The mood in my office was heavy and solemn, mirroring the seriousness of what was ahead. Every decision, every procedure, every effort had led us here. I steadied myself for the mayhem, knowing that no amount of preparation could truly soften its impact.

I sent for her. A simple request passed from me to the nurse, and then to Elena: "J. Alexander wants to see you in his office." The words felt almost too small for what was about to happen, yet they carried the weight of every decision, every conversation, every frustrated attempt to reach her. I waited, knowing she would appear at any moment, bracing myself for the intensity that always accompanied her presence. I sat in my chair, rehearsing my words carefully: "Elena, we can't continue your stay here. You're being discharged." A soft knock came at the door. "Please come in," I said deliberately. "And close the door."

It didn't take a single word beyond that. She had been here before, and she could read the mixed emotions stretching across my face. She knew. Every step she took toward the chair carried the weight of previous consequences, written warnings, and emotional storms. As she settled into the seat across from me, the room seemed to shrink, and I braced myself for the tidal wave I was certain would follow.

The moment she was secure in the chair, her reaction detonated. The armor she had worn since her arrival shattered. She sobbed uncontrollably—body trembling, face streaked with tears. Her hands clawed at the edge of the chair as if trying to hold herself together. My guard rose immediately. *Manipulation,* I thought. *Here it comes.* The shifting of blame. The twisting of words. The emotional bait designed to pull me in just far enough to feel responsible for her pain. I readied myself for the turn—the sudden shift from victim to accuser, the rewriting of our last exchange, the subtle push-and-pull that turns empathy into guilt. I'd seen it before: the desperate need to control the narrative, to make our program the villain so she wouldn't have to face the chaos inside herself.

But the Elena I was prepared for wasn't the Elena who showed up in my chair that day. There was no accusation, no twisting, no blame. What poured out of her wasn't strategy—it was hopeless surrender. Between gasps, her words came out fragmented and raw, stripped of calculation. "I'm so tired," she whispered. "I don't know how to be this person anymore." Then something in her voice cracked open—desperate and sharp. "You can't leave me!" Fear and fury tangled in the sound. "Nobody ever stays. Nobody cares! I came here for help, but no one understands. I need the help—I know I do. I'll do anything. Anything you say. Just… please don't discharge me." The fight in her eyes was gone, replaced by something childlike—terrified and pleading. In that moment, the truth became unmistakable: this wasn't manipulation; this was survival. The breakdown wasn't an act—it was the collapse of someone who had spent too long holding the world together with nothing but fear and sheer will.

Her desperation filled the room. Every word, every sob, every tremor carried the chaos she lived with—the fear of abandonment, the relentless intensity of her emotions, the fierce longing to be understood, seen, and held, even as she doubted anyone could truly do it. Her words lingered in the air, heavy and unrelenting. The emotion was raw, unstable, and terrifying—but familiar. She wasn't performing; she was unraveling, driven by the same currents of panic and need that define the borderline struggle: a desperate plea not to be left alone inside the storm.

I couldn't speak, even as I recognized this might be a turning point for change. But did that matter? The decision had already been made. Could I risk not discharging her? Could I send her back to the street believing this was a pivotal moment? A million questions raced through my mind at once—safety, responsibility, the well-being of staff and clients, and the fragile thread of hope that maybe, just maybe, she could finally receive what she needed. I sat in silence, emotions swirling, the weight of the moment pressing down.

Every second felt heavy with possibility and risk. This could be the breakthrough—the opening she had been reaching for—but doubt gnawed at me: what if I was wrong? What if this moment didn't lead anywhere? What if I was misreading the moment, or worse, being pulled in by manipulation? The dissonance between my head and my heart felt like it was tearing me in half, leaving me suspended in uncertainty, knowing the next move could define everything.

I broke my silence with a single word. "Anything?" I asked. My voice was calm but steady, carrying the weight of the moment. "Yes," she replied, her voice trembling but firm enough to signal she was listening—ready and willing to engage. "I don't know if we can continue to work with you. I need a few minutes to think about this," I said, letting my words settle. "Please go back to your room. I'll come get you."

Elena nodded, hesitated for just a moment, and then slowly rose and left the office. The silence that followed was heavy, almost tangible, as I sat there processing the intensity of what had just occurred. Every instinct screamed to act, to fix, to control—but I knew this pause was necessary. This silence was part of the process, part of the bridge we were about to build.

Indescribable emotions scattered through my mind, each one jostling the next like restless waves. My nerves felt taut, buzzing beneath my skin—a mix of anticipation, apprehension, and that quiet tremor that comes when you sense something pivotal is about to happen. Every sense was heightened, every thought looping between sureness and doubt, fear and possibility.

Grounding. Breathing. Coping. My mind screamed for a pause, a moment to steady itself amid the storm. I needed time to think, to process, to find my footing before stepping back into the intensity. Each inhale was a tether; each exhale, a minor release. But the questions, the doubts, the anticipation—they lingered, circling like restless shadows in the back of my mind.

Ten minutes felt like ten days, each second stretching, weighted with tension and uncertainty. But a decision had to be made. I couldn't stay suspended in hesitation; the moment demanded clarity, action, and the courage to step into the unknown. I pulled a pad from my desk drawer and a pen from its tray, drawing a line down the middle of the page. On one side, I wrote "Keep"; on the other, "Discharge." No other words were needed. I set the pen down—the choice had been made.

I knew it would not be well-received by staff or clients. I chose not to discharge Elena. It was risky, yes, but I had a specific plan in mind—a way to contain the chaos, address her intense emotions, and create an opening for real work to begin. The weight of the choice pressed on me, but beneath it, a glimmer of possibility stirred. I believed this was the breakthrough she needed. I also knew I would have to meet with staff and be prepared for the backlash of concerns and complaints. I was never the type of clinical supervisor to make demands, but this was different. I needed to hold my ground.

I called an impromptu meeting to inform staff about my decision. As expected, their reactions were a mix of skepticism, hesitation, and open reluctance. Some shook their heads, others crossed their arms, and a few avoided eye contact entirely. I explained what had happened in my last encounter with Elena; they couldn't see what I had seen in that moment—the smallest opening, the rare chance for a breakthrough—but I understood their doubts. The responsibility of this decision rested solely on my shoulders. I knew I had to proceed with care, every step deliberate, every word measured.

We sat together, honest and unguarded, discussing risks, contingencies, and the support Elena would need. Questions flew quickly, concerns were voiced, and tension filled the room—but by the end, there was a reluctant understanding. They saw, however faintly, that this wasn't just about rules or protocol; it was about seizing a rare opportunity for real change. All I asked of my staff was to trust the process.

I asked the staff to wait until I had spoken with Elena directly before sharing anything with the other clients. I laid out the parameters in my mind: if she was willing to follow the plan and work with my guidance, she could stay. If not, she could choose to leave. The decision would ultimately be hers, but I needed to create space for her to see the opportunity—and for me to know whether she was ready to take it. The staff agreed to continue their day as planned until notified.

I dismissed them and walked down the hall to get Elena. My emotions were steady, anchored by the clarity of my purpose. The plan was concrete, mapped out in my mind, every step considered. Still, tension hummed beneath the surface. I knew I could be wrong and that I might still need to discharge her. But at the very least, giving Elena a choice felt right—it felt humane.

I knocked gently on her bedroom door and spoke her name softly. "Elena," I said, "I'm ready to see you in my office." From the other side, I heard the faint sound of her wiping tears from her face. She had been crying since she left my office. "That's a good sign," I told myself. She is experiencing real emotion. Each sound echoed the storm inside her—the trembling, the fear, the raw vulnerability that always lived just beneath the surface, now magnified.

We walked down the hallway side by side without speaking. The silence was heavy but not empty—filled with anticipation, tension, and an unspoken understanding between us. With each step toward my office, the hallway seemed to lengthen and narrow. *Anything*. Such a simple word, yet so powerful. We entered the office, closed the door, and sat down. Before confirming my decision, I asked again, "You said you're willing to do anything?"

She nodded—a small gesture, but resolute. I took a slow breath, grounding myself. "I'm going to give you a choice," I said. "If you feel you can agree to the plan I lay out and follow through, you can stay. If not, we'll have to proceed with the discharge." It was an ultimatum, but one that returned a measure of power in a situation where she often felt powerless.

Her heel bounced rapidly as I began laying out the plan. "First," I said, "I want all the clients to be able to express their concerns, their thoughts, and their feelings. We'll call this a community feedback circle. They need to say what's on their minds, and you need to hear it."

She gasped. I continued, "They will need to do so uninterrupted." Fear washed over her immediately. I knew what she was imagining—another moment of rejection, another situation where the group might turn on her. I reached out gently. "I will sit next to you. I will ensure the group stays on track and refrains from abusive language. But they need to be able to communicate."

She sat closed off, small, hands folded in her lap, eyes on the floor.

"Next," I said, "I will be your primary counselor. I will work with you directly, and I want you to be open to trying to resolve some of your trauma." For a moment, she didn't move—then, slowly, I saw it: a flicker in her eyes, a soft release in her shoulders, a tentative willingness to reach toward something steadier than the chaos she lived in. "If you can agree to these two conditions," I continued, "you can stay. We'll discuss the rest later." The words hung between us, charged with possibility, and for the first time, she seemed to consider that maybe she didn't have to face everything alone.

She nodded, a clear sign of agreement. I moved immediately to put the plan into action. I called all counselors, staff, and clients into the group room, arranged two chairs at the front, and sat Elena beside me, facing the rest of the room. All eyes were on us, the air thick with tension and anticipation.

For a small room packed with about thirty-five people, not a sound could be heard—so quiet you could hear a pin drop on the carpet. I spoke clearly and confidently, explaining the rules of the group and setting the stage with deliberate intention. Every word was chosen carefully, every pause measured.

This wasn't just about structure; it was about creating a safe container where honesty could emerge without fear, where Elena could experience being heard without chaos or judgment.

The room remained silent for a moment—or two—that felt like an eternity. Then, unexpectedly, Elena spoke first, offering an apology and an attempt to make amends. I had not anticipated this. Shocked and moved, I held back my own tears as I watched her try—imperfectly, shakily—to apologize without rationalizing her behavior. Her words were uneven, but the intention behind them was unmistakable. In that moment, sincerity mattered more than skill, and everyone could feel it.

I glanced at the counseling staff, silently acknowledging the breakthrough. There was no applause, no dramatic shift—just a subtle step toward accountability, a change in the room's energy that spoke louder than anything said out loud. For the first time, her vulnerability met her courage, and that alone reminded everyone present that real change begins not with perfection but with the willingness to try.

I had followed a clinical hunch that things would stabilize once the plan was in motion, but what happened next exceeded my expectations. Clients began to speak. And instead of condemnation, Elena was met with encouragement. Rather than frustration, their concerns sounded like, "We don't know what's happening, but we want you in this group," and, "We enjoy having you here; doing chores with you makes the house feel complete."

One by one, clients expressed a desire for connection, inclusion, and recognition of their presence in the community. Their words flowed—hesitant at first, then more confident—each statement a bridge, each acknowledgment a thread weaving Elena back into the fabric of the group. Among the positive responses were voices from those who had been hurt the most. Their feedback was raw and honest: "I feel unhappy when I have to do your chore because you don't do it. It's not fair for everyone else. Nobody wants to do chores, but we all do." And another, "I feel frightened when you slam doors and scream down the hallway. It puts me on edge, and I feel the urge to run away from this place." Throughout it all, Elena made a concerted effort not to argue with her peers. She nodded and listened.

I looked around the room and saw my clinical staff's reluctance beginning to fade. Their shoulders loosened, their expressions shifting from skepticism to cautious curiosity. Even my own hesitation—the doubt gnawing at me since the moment I made the decision—began to ease. The energy in the room was changing; something fragile, tentative, yet profoundly real was starting to take root.

The group ended in a swirl of tears, smiles, and tentative hugs. Relief, connection, and the faint beginnings of trust lingered in the air. But I knew the work was far from over. The breakthrough in that room was only the beginning. The real work—the deep, deliberate, and often painful work of change and healing—was beginning. For now, that small sense of progress would carry us into the next day. It was a tiny victory, a temporary bridge over the chaos, and just enough to keep hope alive—for Elena, for the group, and for me. Tomorrow, the deeper work would begin. But for that moment, we had survived together.

When I arrived the following morning, a shift in the atmosphere was immediately noticeable. There was a lightness in the air, a subtle easing of tension that hadn't existed in weeks. Conversations carried a softer tone, movements were less guarded, and even the smallest gestures hinted at a renewed sense of possibility. The residential house felt different—not perfect, not resolved—but alive with the potential for change.

I had an unresolved conversation with Elena, and I felt the need to capitalize on the forward progress. We needed to discuss the work we were about to begin—work that was layered, personal, and emotionally demanding. I called her back to my office. When she arrived, she was noticeably different—there was a lightness in her step, a cautious openness in her posture, a positive energy that hadn't been there before. It was a small but meaningful shift, the first sign that yesterday's breakthrough had begun to take hold.

As a budding therapist at the start of my practicum, there were things I could and could not do. Specific therapeutic interventions were off-limits until I had proper training, and some were untouchable until I was fully licensed. I was mindful of these boundaries, yet my mind couldn't help but reach beyond them, searching for ways to connect with the clients who sat across from me. With guidance from my clinical supervisor, I began shaping something of my own— an approach I called *The Process of Healing*.

It wasn't a manualized treatment or textbook technique; it was a framework born out of observation, empathy, and the handful of skills I could ethically and safely use. I had "Frankensteined" this intervention together, piece by piece. Over time, it took shape—a blend of rapport-building, gentle reframing, grounding techniques, psychoeducation, and exercises designed to help clients step toward their pain without being consumed by it. It was still young—like me—but it was something I believed in. None of the individual interventions was uniquely my own; instead, they were a collection of approaches I had seen work on their own, now woven into a single, structured framework.

I discussed *the Process for Healing* with Elena. She seemed intrigued and receptive to the interventions I proposed. I knew we didn't have much time to work—her stay here was a clock ticking loudly in the corner of every session, each minute held hostage by funding timelines. So, I went straight to the heart of it. I told her we weren't just going to talk about her pain. Talk therapy seldom holds the keys to freedom, and treatments without structure can do more harm than good. Over the next several weeks, we would walk through her story step by step in a way that gave her control. I laid out the process as if I were showing her a map: first, we would piece together the history of what had happened—not to dwell, but to understand the story in its full shape. Then we would build a safe space together, using the five senses to make it so vivid she could almost smell the air and feel the ground beneath her feet.

We would delve deep into psychoeducation. I wanted her to understand that trauma isn't just a memory; it is a survival pattern etched into the body, a physical imprint that rewrites the rules of safety and trust. And when she was ready, we would reach the final stage—the Gestalt empty chair—where the ghosts of her past could finally be spoken to, confronted, and, if we were fortunate, left behind. It wasn't magic, but it was the closest thing I had to a map out of the dark.

Elena kept her end of the bargain. She showed up at my door on time, day after day, ready to work, and I knew that kind of commitment was no small thing for her. As we reviewed her history, the damage was unmistakable—both the wounds inflicted by others and the ones she had carved into herself. We named the people who had shaped her trauma, speaking their names aloud like small exorcisms. She told me about her life in sharp, unapologetic detail—the survival trades she had navigated in the shadowed corners of the night economy, years of bartering her body for safety in ways that left scars deeper than skin. Then came the more profound truth: she had been told her earliest days were marked by the fog of withdrawal, a shadow cast before she could even cry out. It was as if her story had been written before she ever had a chance to hold the pen. She was born with drugs in her system—an infant already in withdrawal.

Over the next week, we moved slowly—deliberately—building her courage brick by brick. I guided her through the safe space exercise, a grounding practice I use to stabilize clients before entering deeper work. I instructed her to begin bilateral tapping, gently alternating her hands on her legs in a left-right rhythm. The motion helps regulate the nervous system, keeping her present while we accessed imagery that might otherwise feel too vulnerable.

As she tapped, I asked her to imagine a place where she felt entirely safe—a real or imagined space that belonged only to her. "Look around in your mind," I said softly. "What do you see?" I gave her time to notice the details—the light, the colors, the way the air moved. Then we explored the senses together. "What do you hear in your safe place? Is there music, the sound of waves, or maybe silence?" I encouraged her to notice what she could smell—the scent of rain, pine, or something familiar that told her she was home. "What can you feel?" I asked. "The ground beneath your feet, the warmth of sunlight, or the cool air on your skin?"

Her breathing deepened as the image took shape, the tension in her shoulders gradually easing. I asked her to stay in that space for a moment and notice the emotions present—not fear or shame, but what lay beneath them: calm, safety, maybe even hope. "This," I told her, "is where we'll always return. When things get heavy, this is where you go." I asked her to open her eyes and walk me through her safe space while I took notes to help guide her if she decompensated during a session.

We were ready. Two weeks of education and preparation—each step careful, almost like walking barefoot through a minefield. During that time, Elena consistently attended groups, ate with peers, and participated fully in all chore activities. Her commitment to herself and the program suggested it was time to revisit her trauma timeline and approach the Empty Chair. I met with my supervisor, and we discussed the rationale for moving forward. By the end of our consultation, we agreed that having more time before entering the intervention would have been ideal; however, Elena's progress, combined with the limited time approved by funding, encouraged us to proceed. Elena would have the final say. She and I met to discuss her thoughts on the progress we had made so far.

During our session, Elena spoke with a determination that had been building since our work began. "It's strange," she said, her eyes fixed somewhere beyond me. "For so long, I thought if I didn't talk about it, it couldn't hurt me. But it's always been there—like a noise I couldn't turn off." She paused, rubbing her palms against her jeans, grounding herself. "I keep seeing their faces, hearing their words. I can't let them keep living in my head. I need to tell them what they did to me… what they took." After another quiet moment, she added, "I need to protect myself the right way."

I reflected on her words. The groundwork had been laid—we had traced the history of her pain, given names and faces to the ghosts that had followed her, and built a safe space strong enough to hold what was coming. She had put in the work.

"I think I'm ready," she said finally. "Not because it doesn't scare me—but because I can't carry it anymore. I need to say it out loud, even if it breaks me."

This wasn't about an exercise or a technique. It wasn't about an empty chair. It was about surrender—allowing herself to confront what had always felt too dangerous to touch. For the first time, she wasn't hiding behind anger or charm or avoidance. She was standing in the truth of what had been done to her. She was ready.

I gave her the autonomy to choose who she wanted to speak to first. Typically, people begin with the person they are angry at—the one who left a wound and never owned it. But not Elena. She wanted to speak to her infant self. It's strange how sitting across from an empty chair can feel like staring into a void. The first rounds of this work are almost always uncomfortable—awkward, tender, a little disorienting. It can also be the most powerful. I stood just behind the empty chair, the room quiet enough to hear the soft tick of the wall clock.

I could sense she was nervous. Her breath was shallow and quick, her posture rigid. "Let's take a few breaths—remember the breathing techniques we practiced," I said. I began breathing slowly and deeply through my nose and exhaling the same way. I continued until Elena's breathing matched mine, and I saw a physical shift in her presence. With my hands, I traced the outline of a cradle in the space above the chair. "This is who you're about to speak to," I told her gently. "Your infant self. Take your time. Be deliberate with your words. See if you can reach for a feeling of strength—even just a thread of it.

The time is yours." I returned to my chair and added softly, "Just pretend I'm not here." I sat in silence as Elena began.

I had used the Empty Chair intervention before, but never as part of my newly formed framework and never for trauma. It had always been linked to addiction. Then Elena did something rare—something I had seen only in the most fragile beginnings of deep work. She quietly stood, slid her chair back, and mimed lifting her infant self from an invisible cradle. She held the imaginary child gently in her arms, then turned her back toward me, shielding the baby from the world. Slowly, she sat down on the floor, holding her infant self close as she rocked ever so slightly.

I couldn't see her face, but I could hear the sound of her tears—the soft, uneven rhythm of her sobs filling the space between us. Her voice trembled as she spoke to the infant she held. She told the child about the world she was about to enter, warning her of the pain she would be asked to endure before she even had the words to name it. She spoke of the misunderstandings that would twist themselves into her young heart, teaching her—far too early—that she didn't quite belong. She whispered about the moments when she would feel invisible, detached from those around her, and how that loneliness would settle in like a shadow she could never outrun.

Her words carried a heartbreaking mix of sorrow and love—a desperate wish to protect the child in her arms from everything she herself had endured, even while knowing she couldn't change the story that had already been written.

I sat in my chair behind my desk, trying to stay unnoticed, breath shallow and heart tight. The room felt simultaneously vast and impossibly small, charged with a tension I could almost touch. Every word, every tremor in her body, tugged at something deep in me—a blend of fear, awe, and something dangerously close to hope, freedom, and genuine acceptance. I could feel her pain filling the space between us, yet beneath it was the emerging sense of something unexpectedly beautiful: a child held, a voice finally permitted to speak, a story being witnessed.

For a long moment, I did nothing but listen, letting the world shrink to the sound of her voice and the rhythm of her sobs. I realized that what was happening wasn't just therapy. It was sacred. It was trust. And it was the first step in a journey that might finally allow her—and the little girl inside her—to breathe.

As the minutes passed, her sobs softened, the raw tremor in her voice settling into something steadier. She rocked the child gently, pausing between sentences as though listening for a reply she could not yet hear. Then, almost imperceptibly, her tone began to shift. Where there had been only fear and warning, now there was a whisper of reassurance—a promise she didn't fully believe yet but desperately wanted to offer.

"You're going to be okay," she whispered, rocking the infant closer. "I… I will try to protect you. I can't make it perfect, but I'll do my best." Her words stumbled over themselves—uncertain, awkward—yet there was power in their honesty. I could feel it in the room: the air seemed to lift, just slightly, as if the weight of the past had eased enough to let something new in.

She looked up at the chair, her hands still holding the invisible infant, and for the first time, I saw her shoulders fully relax. She was beginning to meet her own gaze through the lens of compassion. The grief hadn't vanished, and the trauma hadn't been erased, but in that small, trembling voice was a spark of something buried far too long: hope, agency, and the courage to begin rewriting the story of her own life.

It was a subtle shift—easy to miss for anyone not standing there—but I felt it like a tremor beneath my ribs. This was the moment that mattered, the first step out of the storm. And I knew, deep down, that once a person could speak to that part of themselves with care, everything that followed could finally take shape.

Thirty long minutes passed before Elena finished with the infant. When she reached the place where she felt the work was complete, she slowly rose, still cradling and protecting the child as if it were the most fragile thing in the world. She leaned down, kissed the infant gently, and with deliberate care placed the child back into the imaginary cradle. Only then did she return to her chair, sitting with a deep, slow exhale—as if the weight she had carried for so long had lifted, even if only by a fraction.

It took a moment, but when our eyes finally met, it was clear—the experience had to be processed. I asked cautiously, "How do you feel?" She paused, blinking against the lingering weight of tears, and whispered, "Exhausted." And she looked it. Yet behind her eyes was a faint glimmer of joy, a subtle smile rising as if she were experiencing peace for the very first time.

Her voice carried everything her words alone couldn't hold: relief, grief, release, and the raw ache of confronting a part of herself she had hidden in silence for far too long. I nodded and let the pause stretch, giving her the space to feel the enormity of what had just happened.

We spent the next several minutes reflecting—identifying the feelings that surfaced, the memories that had been stirred, and the subtle shifts in her body. I reminded her that it was okay to feel all of it, that this was part of the process: acknowledging pain without letting it consume her, recognizing fear without letting it control her. I asked, "Why the infant first?" She gave a simple but profound answer. "Throughout my life, I don't think I have ever felt protected. I understand that my reactions are unhealthy ways to protect something I can't yet fully understand or explain. I want to start protecting myself in a healthy way."

By the time our reflection ended, she was breathing more steadily, and her posture was more grounded. The exhaustion was still there, but now mingled with something softer—something tentative: the sense that she had taken the first step toward reclaiming a part of herself long buried.

I didn't want to overextend her. The experience needed space and time to settle, to integrate. She had confronted a part of herself most people never meet, and I wanted her to sit with that, to feel the power of it in her own body before moving forward.

After a few moments, I asked, "Do you need to take a nap?"

She exhaled heavily and nodded, a flicker of relief crossing her face. I watched a quiet peace settle over her body as she prepared to rest. "It's a foreign feeling," she said as she rose to her feet. "I can't remember a time when I ever moved freely." She walked slowly toward the door, pausing as she opened it. She inhaled, released a long, steady sigh, offered me a small smile, and disappeared back into her room.

After that Empty Chair session, something shifted in Elena. Her presence felt less guarded, and her engagement in both group and individual work deepened. She participated more openly in exercises, responded thoughtfully in discussions, and showed a budding willingness to confront difficult emotions— even in front of her peers.

Progress wasn't linear—there were still moments of tension, frustration, and tears—but the breakthrough from that first Empty Chair encounter carried her forward. She had experienced what it felt like to be truly seen and heard, and that foundation let us finally build on it.

Weekly concurrent reviews reminded me that time was not on our side. The funding that allowed her to stay was ticking down, a deadline hanging over every session. Each hour carried both promise and pressure, knowing that soon, regardless of readiness, the formal support she depended on would end. Together, we worked to build a bridge that would connect her to continued therapeutic support once she completed.

And then, just like that, her time in the program was over. She had done enough to graduate, sufficient to move forward, but not enough to claim complete healing—no one ever does in such a short time. She chose to move into a sober living environment and continue her treatment through outpatient services, committed to carrying the work forward on her own terms. It was a bittersweet ending to a sour beginning, and the person who walked out was not the same person who had walked in.

In residential treatment, we rarely see the long-term results of the work we put into it. Clients don't often return to thank us—and that's okay. Witnessing their progress in the moment is enough. But with Elena, I had the rare privilege of seeing her again two years later. She had transformed into a remarkable young woman. She had stepped away from the shadowed trades of her past, broken free from toxic cycles, and enrolled in a trade school—her hands now shaping a future instead of surviving the night. She walked in with quiet confidence, the weight of her past still present but no longer defining her.

I was struck silent—a mix of pride, relief, and awe washing over me. Seeing her stand there, fully herself for the first time, brought a deep sense of closure. It wasn't about dramatic breakthroughs or heroic interventions; it was about the small, patient steps, the moments of trust, and the courage to face one's own pain. Elena had done that. She had chosen herself, again and again, and in doing so, she found a life worth living. In that moment, I felt the rare joy of witnessing not just survival but the possibility of true transformation.

Elena's story reminded me—as do the stories of clients who take that first, terrifying step toward healing—that therapy is both unique and profound. It requires a balance of timing, trust, and courage, sometimes resting in the hands of the client and sometimes in the hands of the therapist. In residential treatment, in outpatient care, and in every session held, we are witnesses to human resilience, often in small, almost invisible increments. Elena's journey was a testament to what can happen when someone is truly seen and given the space to confront their pain without judgment. And for me, it reaffirmed why I stay in the chair, why I continue to bear witness, and why—even after all the chaos and heartbreak—I still believe in the possibility of transformation.

CHAPTER 3 - THE TALE OF J. ALEXANDER

Growing Pains

"We are destined to repeat the same mistakes until we finally learn the lessons life insists on teaching us."

"A single look, word, or gesture can ignite tension or trigger old wounds; your presence must anchor the room long before your words ever do."

THE TALE OF J. ALEXANDER

Growing Pains

Growing pains are a part of life. I've had my share—more than I care to count. The truth is, we are destined to repeat the same mistakes until we finally learn the lessons life insists on teaching us. Until then, the cycle continues. Each misstep becomes another chance to grow, to stumble, to rise again, and to try. And every misstep carries weight—sometimes invisible, sometimes unbearably heavy—pressing down in ways that leave a permanent mark.

As a therapist, one of the most valuable lessons I learned came early in my career. It didn't come from a textbook, a lecture, or a training manual, and it hit harder than any theory ever could. It wasn't about technique or procedure—it was about people. About seeing the layers beneath behavior, the armor they wear, and the cracks they hide beneath the surface. It was understanding that sometimes the most meaningful work isn't the information you bring into a group—it's recognizing and responding to the group's needs in that exact moment. It's being flexible, paying attention, and realizing that the best therapy often happens off the page—in the space between words, in silence, and in meeting clients exactly where they are.

I remember it clearly. I had just been hired at a residential program nestled in the rolling hills outside a mid-sized California city. The facility housed a few dozen residents and felt as if it were held together by little more than duct tape and hope. No heaters, no air conditioning—just bare walls, metal bunk beds, and the distant calls of grazing animals across the way. The walls bore the marks of time, the floors were scuffed, the carpet bunched in places, and the asphalt outside was riddled with potholes. And the roof—oh, the roof—cried during storms. Buckets, pots, pans—anything that could catch a drip was pressed into service. No matter how hard the maintenance staff tried, the leaks remained elusive, as stubborn as the men who lived inside. Yet somehow, miraculously, the place passed inspection. It wasn't much, but it felt like home—a chaotic, imperfect space where lives collided, tension hung thick in the air, and where I learned some of the earliest and most enduring lessons of my career.

The men I worked with were street smart, rugged, broken, tattooed, and complicated. Some had spent years surviving on the streets; others were freshly released from prison. At least half were registered sex offenders. Each carried a past weighted with mistakes, trauma, and survival instincts sharpened by a life that rarely offered second chances. Their presence filled the room like an invisible heaviness—palpable, thick in the air—making every breath feel just a little more labored.

By this point in my career, I had moved beyond condemning others' sins. My own healing journey forced me to confront the shadows of my past, teaching me not to punish myself so harshly. Realizing that ultimate judgment rests with God allowed me to step free—free to live without condemnation, and free to extend that same grace to others.

But those lessons, meaningful as they were, weren't the ones this story would teach me. What I was about to encounter would challenge me in a completely different way—less about judgment, more about presence, patience, and the unpredictable, winding paths that real growth often takes.

If you asked my clients, they'd likely say I had a decent bedside manner. Clinically, the term is *unconditional positive regard*—a Rogerian principle. But that phrase doesn't quite capture what it feels like in the room when you're sitting across from someone raw, angry, hurt, or shut down. It's more than a technique; it's a posture. It's showing up fully, holding space without judgment, and letting someone feel seen even when they're screaming, crying, or shutting down. It's the acknowledgment that they exist, that their pain has weight, and that they're allowed to struggle without being defined by the worst parts of themselves.

Doing it one-on-one is challenging enough, but in a group setting, that same unconditional positive regard becomes a high-wire act. You're not just navigating one person's emotions—you're managing a dozen, sometimes more, all colliding in the same space. Each client brings their own trauma, defenses, and agendas, and the energy ricochets from person to person. A single word, a look, or a gesture can ignite tension, trigger old wounds, or set off a chain reaction of emotion. Your ability to stay present—to hold space without judgment, to validate without enabling—is tested in ways that one-on-one sessions rarely demand. It's not just about compassion; it's about vigilance, adaptability, and being quietly strong enough to anchor a room that often feels like it's teetering on the edge of chaos.

The day my lesson unfolded, the edge of chaos didn't just hover—it collapsed in on itself. That sweltering late-summer afternoon pressed down like a forge, the heat climbing into triple digits—the kind of heat that made the air feel thick and alive, pushing against skin and nerves alike. Inside the residential program, the walls felt as if they were closing in, the stale, heavy air mixing with the tension that always seemed to haunt the room. Fans churned but offered little relief. The space smelled of sweat, dust, and a faint chemical tang from cleaning supplies, all blending into a dense, almost tangible haze.

The group began like any other. Men sat shoulder to shoulder on worn benches, sweat tracing lines down their brows, a nervous energy vibrating through their movements—fingers drumming, boots scraping, eyes darting. Restlessness and anxiety mingled in the room, a subtle tension pulsing just beneath the surface. I entered carrying my own agenda, my mind already rehearsing the session I intended to lead. I was lax and distracted—focused more on what I wanted to accomplish than on what was happening right in front of me. I wasn't observing, I wasn't listening. I was present in body, absent in awareness, blind to the undercurrents building quietly around me.

At first, nothing seemed out of the ordinary. The men murmured and shifted in their seats, a few sneaking glances at each other, testing the boundaries of the space. I launched into my planned discussion, the words rolling off my tongue with practiced ease. And then it started—small, almost imperceptible, like the tremor before an earthquake. A snide comment here. A sharp laugh there. An elbow nudge. A muttered "Get off me." The tension I had ignored began to thicken, wrapping around the room like smoke. My carefully crafted agenda evaporated under the weight of the energy I had failed to notice.

With my back turned, scribbling on the whiteboard, the complaints began as a trickle and then a cascade.

"Man, it's hot in here."

"Yo, is there anything you can do?"

I kept writing, hoping it would pass, pretending the rising agitation wasn't building into something more dangerous.

And then—slicing through the drone of murmurs and minor gripes—came the voice from the back corner, sharp, defiant, impossible to ignore.

"Man, FUCK this shit. I'm leaving."

I spun around, heart thudding, eyes wide. Shock rooted me to the spot. The

32

casual chaos I'd been dismissing had detonated into open rebellion. One voice had cut through the tension like a blade, and now every head snapped toward me, waiting—wanting—to see what I would do next.

I stood there, frozen—catatonic—like a statue on display. My inexperience was glaringly obvious, carved into the stiffness of my posture and the blank panic on my face. I watched the client storm toward the door, chest heaving, his words still echoing through the room. *Good one,* I thought bitterly. *Real smooth.* His bravado was both infuriating and impressive—a raw display of power and defiance that left me feeling small, exposed, and utterly unprepared.

Think quick, I told myself, but my brain slogged through molasses. The heat only made it worse; every bead of sweat seemed to drag my thoughts down with it. Before I could form a single word, the mutiny began.

One by one, clients rose from their seats.

"I'm out of here," another barked, slamming his hand against the table.

Then another. And another. Like dominoes falling in rapid succession, the energy of rebellion rippled through the room. Chairs scraped, voices rose in defiance, and I felt the structure of my control crumble in real time. My heart pounded. My mind scrambled. I was losing the group—losing all of them—and with it, the fragile sense of safety I had been trying so hard to maintain.

I raised my voice just above the chaos, reaching for anything—anything—that might halt the stampede. The only thing that surfaced was a threat. One I convinced myself would be harmless.

"The next person who gets up and walks out," I shouted, "will force me to start discharging people and calling parole officers."

For a beat, the room froze. And then, slowly, the weight of what I had just said crashed over me. Nearly three dozen men—men who had survived streets and prison, men trained by life to read danger in a single twitch—were now staring straight at me with focused, almost predatory attention. My words had dropped like stones into a still pond, and the ripples hit harder than I could have imagined. The realization of the power —and the danger—behind what I'd just spoken settled deep in my gut.

But that moment, unnerving as it was, paled in comparison to what I saw

33

next.

My eyes shifted to the client on my right—Marcus. A man whose heritage and history were etched into the deep lines of his face, ink telling stories from neck to knuckles, each piece a survival note from a life tested twice over by the system's weight. And yet, there he was—trembling. Tears streamed down his face in a silent, steady fall. The raw vulnerability in him—so unexpected, so stark—hit me harder than any outburst, any threat, any training manual ever had.

In that instant, the room changed. The chaos hung suspended, every man's energy caught between anger, fear, and something I couldn't immediately name. Recognition, maybe. A shared understanding that, beneath all the armor, none of us was untouchable.

I stood there again, speechless for the second time in that overheated group room—this time for an entirely different reason. The weight of what I had done punched straight through my chest. My words, intended as a harmless boundary, had become poison in the room. I could feel it in the silence, in the stiff postures, in Marcus's shaking shoulders.

It was only then that I knew—we all needed a break. I just as much as they did.

I dismissed the group, letting the men spill outside into the open air, their steps heavy, their voices rising as tension fled their bodies in ways I could feel but couldn't yet fully understand. I slipped back to my office, closed the door behind me, and picked up the phone. Heart racing, hands trembling, I called my supervisor and threw myself under the bus. Every word came out thick with raw honesty—the kind that surfaces when you finally see yourself clearly in the mirror... and don't like the reflection.

I sat in my office, phone pressed to my ear, feeling every ounce of gravity in the moment—solemn, tearful, heart hammering. On the other end, my supervisor's voice cut through the tension like sunlight breaking through a storm—lighthearted, teasing, and calm.

"J," he said with a dry chuckle, "welcome to the joys of growing pains. You're learning. Every misstep is part of the process. But make no mistake— you created a mess, and now you get to clean it up."

His words carried both reassurance and truth. A shaky laugh escaped me, because as heavy as it all felt, I knew he was right. This was the kind of lesson no textbook could prepare you for—the messy, chaotic, unforgettable kind that only real practice can teach.

Before we hung up, he and I unpacked the deeper teaching buried beneath the chaos. We talked about the danger of becoming too rigidly attached to an idealized plan for group work—being so focused on curriculum, schedules, or state-agency expectations that you miss the needs of the people right in front of you.

"Sometimes," he said, "the most therapeutic thing you can do is step back, acknowledge what's happening in the room, and give the group a break—especially when the conditions are extreme. That's where real growth starts."

I let the words settle, feeling both the weight and the relief of his wisdom. It wasn't in any academic lecture or supervision manual. It was raw, lived, messy—and absolutely necessary.

But that was only the first lesson. The next one came after I faced what I had created.

For the next two days, I conducted what were supposed to be one-on-one sessions with nearly three dozen clients. But they weren't really "sessions." They were amends—individual moments of accountability where I apologized without excuses and set an expectation for myself to do better. Each conversation was a chance to acknowledge my mistake, repair the rupture, and rebuild trust.

I listened. I owned my errors. I made sure each client knew I saw them, respected them, and understood that they were allowed to struggle without being defined by their worst moment. And I made it clear that I expected the same grace in return.

It was grueling, humbling work—yet essential. In the process, I learned that accountability, like therapy itself, isn't about ego. It's about presence, repair, and the willingness to show up again after you've fallen short.

The day after I finished the individual amends, I brought all the men of the house together for a full group session, this time in the cooler hours of the afternoon. I asked every staff member to join as well, creating a space where clients and staff alike could witness the moment of accountability.

I made one final, deliberate statement—acknowledging the chaos of the previous week, owning my missteps without softening them, and emphasizing the lessons we could carry forward together. The atmosphere was tense but contained, charged with a blend of curiosity, relief, and cautious respect.

As the days went on, I began to notice subtle shifts. The raw edges of the previous incident softened, giving way to a more profound sense of mutual respect between me and the clients. What had erupted as chaos had unexpectedly opened a door—a chance to model what healthy accountability looks like. Owning mistakes, apologizing without defensiveness, and making amends. And the clients responded in kind.

Conversations grew more genuine. Group engagement became more deliberate. Even small acts of responsibility carried new meaning. It was a living lesson in the power of presence, humility, and consistency. The work wasn't over—far from it—but for the first time, I could feel trust beginning to take root.

Reflecting on the experience, I realized the true lesson behind growing pains: life, like therapy, is a relentless teacher. Mistakes are inevitable. Chaos is unavoidable. And yet every stumble carries the seed of growth. The courage isn't found in avoiding the fall—it's in how you rise, how you acknowledge your missteps, and how you show up again, fully present and fully human.

In that small, imperfect group room, surrounded by broken yet resilient men, I learned something I would carry with me forever: healing, growth, and trust are never neat or predictable. They are messy. They are demanding. And they are beautiful in their imperfection.

CHAPTER 4 - THE TALE OF MARK

On the Edge

"In this line of work, sometimes we are not meant to finish the story. Our role is to witness, act where we can, and carry the weight of the unknown with as much grace as possible."

"Even the best intentions cannot save every life. And yet the effort—the care, the vigilance—matters every single time."

THE TALE OF MARK

On the Edge

It would be ideal if every therapeutic interaction ended in healing, clarity, or forward movement. But that isn't the truth. In this work, we witness victories—moments of breakthrough, recovery, and hope. Yet for every one of those moments, others leave you unsettled, replaying them long after the session has ended. In substance abuse counseling, the line between hope and tragedy is razor-thin, and you learn quickly that your job is to stand inside that tension without letting it break you. You carry the weight of your clients' choices—their progress and their regressions—even when none of it is genuinely yours to bear. Every moment, every decision, every word spoken or left unsaid can ripple outward in ways you never see coming.

Some clients walk into your office carrying stories you don't forget. Not everyone moves steadily from week to week; not everyone grows in clean, predictable lines. Some arrive in turmoil, dragging a storm behind them that leaves you shaken long after they're gone. Their presence lingers—not because of triumph, but because of how close they came to the edge. And sometimes what haunts you most is not knowing whether they stepped back to safety or slipped quietly into the fall. These are the stories you carry—the ones that shape your sense of caution, purpose, and empathy. They become composites drawn from many lives, blurred at the edges to protect the fragile thread of trust. In those softened outlines, one story becomes a mirror for a dozen more—each with its own fractures, its own near-misses with the abyss.

Mark arrived during a sweltering summer a few years back. His battle with alcohol was relentless—so consuming that he'd survived severe withdrawal multiple times before. These episodes weren't just tremors and confusion; they were seizures, hallucinations, cardiac danger—even the kind of withdrawal that kills if you're unlucky or untreated. Mark walked that tightrope every day. Even in casual conversation, a nervous tension buzzed beneath his words, a restless desperation he struggled to contain. His history was marked by near-disasters—moments where his body and mind nearly surrendered to alcohol's grip—and yet somehow he kept surviving. But each new day brought the same deadly gamble.

During intake, we completed a full DSM-5 and ASAM assessment, carefully evaluating every facet of his condition. It quickly became clear that his body was at significant risk for withdrawal complications given the severity of his past episodes. Years of heavy drinking had already compromised his health, and emotionally, he hovered between depression, anxiety, and unresolved trauma. Stress overwhelmed him easily, and his wavering motivation left him vulnerable to relapse at any time.

His story wasn't unique. It echoed the desperation of countless others who had sat in that same chair—people whose addictions had eroded not only their bodies but the scaffolding of their everyday lives: the mechanic whose calloused hands now trembled over tools he once commanded with confidence; the teacher whose voice cracked mid-lesson, silenced by a bottle that refused to loosen its hold.

Mark's environment offered no real support, and the people he could rely on were few—mirroring the isolation so many clients face when they walk through our doors. Taken together, the picture was unmistakable: he needed immediate withdrawal management followed by residential treatment. Though he initially requested outpatient care, the clinical reality made it clear that a higher level of support was essential for both his safety and any hope of sustained recovery. We explained that treatment couldn't move forward if he arrived under the influence—and that if he did, residential care would be the only responsible next step. He understood.

Before he ever walked in for his first session, the office buzzed with an unspoken tension. We had reviewed his notes, studied his history, and knew what kind of storm we were preparing for. Even as seasoned counselors, you feel it—the electric charge in the air when a client like this is expected. There's anticipation, yes, but also dread. You rehearse every possible scenario: What if he's stable? What if he's not? What if he escalates beyond control? It's a delicate balance between preparedness and humility. You can't control the storm—you can only decide how you're going to stand in it.

Based on his assessment, we knew his behavior would be unpredictable. Some days, he showed up calm, open, and ready to engage. Other days, he disappeared for weeks without a trace. And when he did return, he carried the storm with him—a volatile mix of desperation, withdrawal, and unresolved pain that echoed the struggles of so many walking the same razor's edge. Outpatient treatment had been his choice, and although we knew residential care offered the best chance at survival, we met him where he was. In the rhythm of his brief arrivals and long vanishings, I recognized the familiar cadence of relapse—a dance of determination and defeat, where every step forward is shadowed by the gravity of old habits waiting to pull you back under.

One afternoon, he came through our door unannounced. The reception area was quiet. He burst in, slamming the door so hard it bounced off the wall, shouting and demanding to be seen. His eyes darted wildly—bloodshot and unfocused—scanning the room as if outrunning something only he could see. His speech came in slurred fragments, broken by sobs, gasps, and jagged breaths. His body swayed under the weight of impending collapse.

Before anyone could intervene, he lurched behind the reception desk, shoving paperwork aside and dropping into the chair as if it were the only anchor keeping him tethered to reality. Words tumbled out in frantic, incoherent bursts—paranoia bleeding into half-formed hallucinations, all of it fused with a desperate cry for help. Objects rattled as he gestured wildly, knocking over wastebaskets and pushing shelves off balance. At one point, he flipped desk organizers, scattering pens, clips, and paperwork across the counter like pieces of a life coming undone.

I recognized it instantly: he was sliding into severe alcohol withdrawal—delirium tremens tightening its grip. It's a storm both familiar and fearsome in this line of work, one I've seen shadow more thresholds than I can count. And as he spiraled, the room itself seemed to shrink, pulled inward by the gravity of his disorientation and the unmistakable danger of a man perched on the edge of self-destruction.

I was torn—caught between the instinct to move toward him and the instinct to retreat. Every part of me screamed in both directions at once. One side wanted to steady him, to guide him back from the precipice he was slipping toward. The other recognized the danger—the volatility in his movements, the unpredictability in his eyes—and knew that one wrong step could ignite a spiral I wouldn't be able to contain. I tried to speak, but my throat was dry, my words lodged halfway between intention and fear.

Stay calm. Breathe. Don't touch him. Stay present, I told myself.

The creeping worry—the very real fear of seizures, collapse, or death—pressed to the front of my mind. This wasn't just emotional instability; this was a medical crisis unfolding in real time. I weighed every possibility in seconds, each heartbeat a reminder that a single miscalculation could turn catastrophic.

That fear became my compass. It steadied me just enough to think clearly, to balance compassion with caution in a moment that demanded both.

Leaving him slumped in the chair, eyes wild and unfocused, I sprinted down the hallway to find the office manager. One glance at my face and he understood—no explanation needed. This was an emergency.

He followed me back to the front, and together we snapped into action. Without speaking, we split the responsibilities. I grabbed the phone, dialing emergency services with trembling hands, staying close enough to monitor him without crowding his space. The office manager stepped outside to meet the responders, ready to guide them straight into the storm that was consuming our front office.

The room vibrated with urgency. Every second stretched thin, every heartbeat a reminder that time was working against us and that the slightest misstep could tip the moment into disaster.

The wait for help was only three minutes, but each second dragged like an eternity. He continued to unravel with alarming speed. He tore at his clothes in frantic bursts until a hidden flask tumbled onto the carpet. He spat on the floor, his movements jerking and disorganized. Then he slid out of the chair entirely, clawing at the carpet as though trying to anchor himself to something only he could see. Drool pooled beneath him, a physical manifestation of a mind losing its grip.

His sobs deepened into guttural cries—raw, primal, unrestrained. He called out to long-lost loved ones, confessing distorted memories and old guilt in broken fragments that spilled from him like shards. The room felt as if it were shrinking around him, his world collapsing inward as I faded further and further from his perception. Every shadow startled him, every sound amplified his panic. It was chaos embodied—a living, breathing storm.

Time hung suspended. I watched every twitch, every tremor, every panicked flick of his eyes, feeling both powerless and tethered to the fragile thread of his consciousness. My mind spun through worst-case scenarios: What if he seized? What if the hallucinations turned violent? What if he collapsed before help arrived? Papers lay scattered across the floor, chairs shoved aside, shelves jarred loose, the spilled flask glinting on the carpet—the room itself becoming a mirror of his internal rupture. I spoke to him softly, repeatedly, trying to offer an anchor to the present. But to him, I no longer existed.

When the responders finally arrived, we guided them in and stepped back. At first, he accepted their presence, but the moment he moved toward the door and caught sight of the vehicle, panic detonated. His voice cracked as he screamed, "Not the authorities! I'm not going away!" Every inch they tried to guide him toward the ambulance was met with frantic resistance.

His body twisted violently, limbs flailing as if fighting off reality itself. Even as we spoke gently, our words were swallowed by the sheer terror pouring out of him. The fear etched into his face was unmistakable. He wasn't fighting us— he was fighting the collapse of his world. I had seen shades of this in other unravelings: that raw instinct to flee confinement, to outrun the invisible chains of shame and survival that bind tighter than any restraint ever could.

The responders froze for a moment, stunned by the intensity. Their eyes darted between him and us, each step cautious, every movement calculated to avoid triggering a deeper collapse. And then he bolted. His scream split the air as he ran—past us, past the responders, past the ambulance—his panic leaving a trail of fear, confusion, and heartbreak in its wake.

In that instant, everything slowed—the screech of shoes on asphalt, the frantic calls from the responders, the helpless catch in our own breaths—each sound underscoring the brutal reality that he was gone, and nothing we had tried could tether him back. In his terror, his unraveling, I felt a deep ache for him—a man trapped inside a body and mind he could no longer control, fleeing from the very help that might have saved him.

And just like that, he was gone. The ambulance doors closed on an empty power cot, and the spot he had occupied moments before felt hollow, vacuumed of air. The echoes of his screams clung to the walls, vibrating through the stillness he left behind. We stood in stunned silence—hearts pounding, adrenaline still surging—while the responders exchanged uncertain glances, unsure how to document what had unfolded. The weight of helplessness settled in my chest like a stone. There was no triumph here—only fear, questions, and the haunting uncertainty of whether he had found safety or slipped deeper into the spiral we had tried so hard to pull him from. That question remains with me even now.

Some clients walk away with hope. Some find healing. And some slip through the cracks, leaving behind nothing but the ache of what might have been. Mark was one of those. Even weeks later, the memory of him lingered in the quiet corners of the office—the echo of his screams, the storm of his last moments, the raw vulnerability in his eyes. For the staff, his absence became a stark reminder that no amount of preparation, empathy, or training guarantees a safe outcome. For me, he became an unanswered question: had he found a foothold on the edge, or had he fallen into the darkness we feared for him?

In the days that followed, we debriefed again and again. Each of us processed the chaos differently—some in silence, some with shaky laughter, all of us replaying the moment in our minds. I scrutinized every detail, every decision, wondering whether there was another path, another option, another version of myself that might have changed the outcome. Eventually, reality settled in: in this work, sometimes we are not meant to finish the story. Our role is to witness, to act where we can, to hold steady in the uncertainty, and to carry the weight of the unknown with as much grace as we can muster.

That, perhaps, is the actual lesson—one learned not in classrooms, but in the raw, unfiltered reality of the work. Even the best intentions cannot save every life. And yet the effort—the care, the vigilance, the readiness—matters every single time. These moments, etched into the collective memory of our field, remind us of the oath we take: not to recount a single fate, but to illuminate the shadowed weave of recovery itself. Each anonymous life, each blurred composite, teaches us something essential.

And in the aftermath of storms like this one, we gather the shards—not just from this moment, but from the countless tempests before and the ones still ahead—reminding ourselves that every echo is a call to hold space wider, to listen deeper, for the ones who circle back... and for those who never do.

CHAPTER 5 - THE TALE OF RAVEN

New Beginnings

"Progress is never linear; patience, persistence, and empathy are as critical as any plan or intervention."

"Every story, no matter how unfinished, leaves a mark."

THE TALE OF RAVEN

New Beginnings

I had been working at a non-profit outpatient facility for about a year. Building a caseload in a non-profit program was never a challenge—clients came in steadily through a call center. Referrals would land on the admissions organizer's desk, and from there, they ensured clients were distributed evenly among staff to help maintain balanced caseloads. Most of the time, it was random, though there were exceptions. A Spanish-speaking client would see a bilingual clinician, and sometimes clients request a counselor of the same gender. My referrals, however, often carried another pattern: if a client was known to have significant mental health needs, they were usually routed to me—echoing the rhythms of so many who arrive with layered shadows trailing behind, searching for even the faintest promise of steadiness.

One morning, the admission organizer walked into my office carrying a thick stack of papers. She didn't need to say a word—her expression gave her away. She was about to hand me one of those cases. The kind where a client had cycled through treatment more than once, never able to hang on to hope long enough to sustain change. She set the file down and said, "We'll give you this client, but you need to know a little bit about her past. She's returned to programs like ours multiple times. Struggles every time, then leaves treatment before the work can even begin." The organizer paused before adding, "For more information, you should talk to the program director when she gets in. She was the last one to work with her."

That afternoon, I picked up the admissions packet and trudged slowly down the hall to the director's office. Her door was open. I knocked and asked if she had time for a consultation. "Sure," she said, motioning me in. I sat down across from her desk, hesitated for a moment, and then said just one word: the client's name. I didn't need to say more. The reaction unfolded on the director's face like a story all its own—hope, frustration, humor—all flickering across before she could form a single word. I leaned back, let out a breath, and simply said, "Wow." It was the only word that felt big enough to hold what her expression had already told me.

The director dropped her hands from the keyboard and leaned back in her chair, mirroring my posture, exhaling like the name itself carried a weight she'd been holding too long. "She's tough," she finally said. "Not because she's mean, not because she fights the process—but because stimulants set off these psychotic breaks. One moment she's with you, the next she's deep in a full-blown conversation with the filing cabinets, like they've got all the answers she's looking for. Then she disappears. Vanishes from the program, from herself. And when she comes back, it's like pressing reset. You're sitting across from someone who's half stranger, half ghost. You wonder if this time you'll find the thread that holds her together long enough to make it count—a pattern woven from the lives of so many women who teeter on these flimsy edges, their storms as individual as they are familiar, yet bound by the same quiet ache to be understood."

The director rubbed her temples like she was sorting through memories that didn't belong to her but had left their fingerprints all over her. "The thing is," she continued, "when she's clear, she's sharp. Smarter than she gives herself credit for. She'll sit in the group, break down someone else's story with this clarity that makes the whole room go quiet. And then—snap—just like that, she's back in her own world. Talking to shadows, holding conversations with beings that aren't there, bargaining with ghosts only she can see. It's like watching a storm roll in on a clear day—you know it's coming, but you're never quite ready for how hard it hits, no matter how many times you've seen her weather shift."

She shook her head and gave a small laugh, though it wasn't out of humor. "I guess what makes her challenging isn't the stimulants or even the psychosis. It's the way she makes you hope. Every time she comes back, you can't help but think maybe this time it'll stick. Perhaps this time she'll stay on the side of herself that's fighting to live. And then she's gone again, and you're left sitting here wondering how many more chances she has left before hope itself runs out.

The director's gaze drifted past me, fixed on nothing, like she was replaying a reel only she could see. "You'll know her the second she walks in," she said quietly. "It's not the clothes, not the way she talks—it's the eyes. There's always something behind them, moving, restless, like you're never the only one in the room with her. She'll talk to file cabinets like they're old friends, carry on conversations that no one else can hear—and yet, somehow, she'll make it feel natural, like maybe you're just late to the dialogue, a guest arriving mid-sentence to a story she's been living for years."

She paused, then gave a small smile, almost conspiratorial. "But here's the thing—where some therapists back away, I think you'll lean in. The way you work, the patience you have with letting people unfold at their own pace—I can see it being exactly what she needs. Most therapists try to pin her down, box her symptoms, and keep her on track. You've never been like that. You listen differently. And if anyone can cut through the static she lives in, it might just be you." The director leaned forward, resting her elbows on the desk. "So, when she shows up, be yourself."

Her words lingered in the air long after she spoke. I'd been told before that I had a knack for meeting people where they were and rolling with resistance, but hearing it from the director carried a different weight. It wasn't praise—it was an acknowledgment that the next session might turn on the way I showed up, the patience I brought, and the choices I made in real time. Part of me bristled with anticipation, a mix of excitement and apprehension, like stepping toward a doorway without knowing what waits on the other side."

I knew that this client would push boundaries in ways that would challenge my clinical instincts. Yet there was also a spark of hope—mirroring the quiet determinations of so many others who arrive with similar tempests within. Maybe my style—direct, measured, empathetic—was precisely what she needed. I leaned back in my chair, exhaling slowly, letting the tension roll off my shoulders, and just as I started to gather my thoughts, the shuffle of footsteps outside the door caught my attention, pulling me out of the mental script I was already rehearsing for our first moments together."

The office organizer's movements outside the door pulled me from my thoughts. She had come to inform me that Raven was here for her intake appointment. Punctual, I thought—or, perhaps, oriented to time, or maybe someone else was responsible for her timely arrival. My internal monologue continued as my stomach tightened with a familiar mix of nerves and anticipation, the kind that stirs whenever someone with her ferocity steps into the room—reminding me of the dozen others who've tested these same waters. I stood, looked at the director, looked at the office organizer, and with one exhale, we all let out a deep breath as if it were planned, an unspoken acknowledgment of what it means to greet someone whose story arrives before they do."

I followed the office organizer down the hall and into the waiting area. There she was. The first thing I noticed was her posture—willful, stubborn, a kind of tense energy that filled the room. Her hair was disheveled, her clothes mismatched and wrinkled, the faint smell of smoke lingering around her. She was oriented enough to respond when called, but there was an undeniable sense of being out of sorts, as though the world had already pushed back against her before she'd even arrived.

Our eyes met, and I recognized the walls she had built, the armor she wore to keep the world at bay. Yet beneath the defiance, I sensed fragments of vulnerability—small cracks where connection might be possible, echoes of the guarded resilience in clients like her. I greeted her calmly and carefully, keeping my voice steady and measured, and she responded with a hesitant tilt of her head, one eyebrow raised, as if daring me to push too far, too fast. There was a rhythm to her resistance, a pattern I had seen before, and I felt a flicker of confidence that maybe, just maybe, the style I had honed over years of counseling could meet her right where she was, without crowding the fragile space she carried between herself and the world."

I invited Raven back to my office and asked her to take a seat. As she lowered herself into the chair, I reflected on the unpredictability of this work. I knew that every gesture, every pause, every question would matter. What I didn't realize was how long the work would take or what shape it would assume. I braced myself with the reminder I often need when sitting with clients like her: the real work isn't about control—it's about presence, patience, and the willingness to walk alongside someone, even when the path is uncertain, especially when their steps don't match yours. Drawing in a slow breath, I exhaled and began the orientation for the intake session.

Raven sat slouched in the chair, her arms crossed tightly over her chest as though she needed a barrier between herself and the world. Her hair was unkempt, her clothes wrinkled, and her overall appearance suggested a life that had been running rough for some time. Yet beneath the disheveled exterior, she was alert and oriented, her eyes sharp with a kind of guarded defiance. She was willful, stubborn even, and I could feel the push of her resistance in the room before either of us had said much at all. Part of me knew this was her way of testing the space—assessing me. My task, as always, wasn't to break through her defenses but to hold steady, to create a place where she could set them down on her own terms, even only for a moment.

With that in mind, I began to explain the orientation process, careful to pace my words, watching her body language more than her responses, and letting the rhythm of our first exchange begin to take shape. I spoke, Raven rocked gently back and forth in the chair, her eyes fixed on a spot on the floor. I caught myself wondering if any of this was reaching her or if she had already decided it wouldn't work. Don't know if this is going to work, I thought, not about the program itself but about whether she would allow herself to lean into it.

"I've done this before," she muttered, her voice carrying equal parts irritation and weariness. "It never changes anything." I nodded, not arguing, just letting her words hang in the air for a moment. "I hear you," I said calmly. "A lot of people feel that way coming in, especially when it's not their first time at the rodeo." I added, "You don't have to decide today whether this is going to work for you. For now, you're here, so we might as well have a conversation." I stopped talking to avoid filling the air with unnecessary words, giving her room to decide whether she wanted to meet me in the silence.

I watched. Her arms tightened across her chest as if she were hugging herself, but I caught a flicker of thought in her expression. She was contemplating whether or not to make a stand and fight me at this point or open the door a crack for connection. Resistance has its own language—it doesn't always come in words. Sometimes it's a glance away, sometimes a clenched jaw, a quick exhale, a foot tapping, or hands gripping the edges of a chair, each movement revealing more than any sentence could.

It shows up in the way someone leans back or forward, in silence, in hesitation, in the way they avoid or meet your gaze. And sometimes, just sometimes, it's the tiniest twitch of an eyebrow, a barely-there nod, or a softened exhale that whispers the possibility of trust. With Raven, it was all of the above, a symphony of defense and uncertainty playing out across her body and face—but threaded through it was a hint, a subtle signal that beneath the armor, a door was not entirely closed—a language I've learned to read across the faces of so many, where defiance masks the ache of too many false starts and too many exits that felt safer than staying.

In the middle of that joust, I had noticed something: she hadn't left. For all her sharp edges, she was still in the chair, still listening, still choosing—at least for this moment—to stay. And in that simple act, there was the tiniest spark of hope, a subtle reminder that even in resistance, there can be a beginning—much like the tentative openings I've witnessed in so many first encounters, the quiet moment where someone decides not to flee.

The first part of the session passed quietly, not because nothing was happening, but because everything was happening in the small, almost imperceptible spaces between words. Raven didn't volunteer much, and I didn't rush her. Each question I asked was measured, each explanation carefully timed. I let silences hang, knowing that for someone like her, silence could be a shield—but it could also be the space where a choice to trust begins to form.

Every so often, she shifted in her chair, brushing her hair back with her hand, a foot tapping once, twice, then still. I noticed these movements, cataloged them in my mind as small signals, little openings into a world that she didn't easily show anyone. I repeated the fundamental questions of the orientation, not for the answers themselves, but for the rhythm it created— something familiar, predictable, a scaffold for her to lean on if she chose to.

It was a long session. Longer than most first sessions, because we weren't racing toward intake completion or checklists. We were moving at the speed she allowed, weaving in short explanations, gentle clarifications, and moments of acknowledgment when she offered even the slightest sign that she was listening. Occasionally, she muttered under her breath, sometimes disagreeing, sometimes sighing, and sometimes simply noting her presence in the room. Each of these was a thread, fragile but real, the kind that can unravel into connection if handled with care.

By the time the session was nearing its close, we had made a subtle agreement, though neither of us called it that aloud. She would move forward with the rest of the assessment. Not because she had to, not because she was convinced this time would be different, but because in that moment, she had chosen to stay, to engage, to let the process continue on her terms. And in that choice, no matter how small or reluctant, there was the first trace of something that could become trust.

As the clock ticked closer to the usual end of a session, I didn't rush to conclude. Raven hadn't made grand declarations or dramatic shifts, but she was still here—still seated, still breathing, still present. I could feel the tension in her shoulders slowly ease, if only by fractions, and that was enough for now. I summarized what we had covered, not as a checklist, but as a way to acknowledge her participation. "We've made it through this part," I said softly. "That's enough for today."

She didn't smile. She didn't nod, not fully. But she leaned back slightly, uncrossed one arm, and her gaze, though guarded, met mine for just a heartbeat longer than before. It was a small gesture, almost imperceptible, but it was a signal—a subtle recognition that she had been seen, that she had been held through the uncertainty of the session without judgment or pressure. It was the kind of moment that arrives quietly, the kind you only catch if you're paying attention.

As she stood to leave, I noticed the deliberate care in her movements, the slow adjustment of her coat, the gentle brushing of hair from her eyes. She was still stubborn, still wary, but there was a mutual agreement between us, unspoken: we would continue this work, step by step, at the pace she allowed. I walked her to the door, gave her a soft nod, and let the space hold the possibility of tomorrow.

When the office quieted again, I exhaled slowly, feeling the weight of the session settle into my chest—not the heavy weight of chaos, but the careful, tentative weight of a connection that had begun. There were no victories yet, no dramatic breakthroughs, only the insubstantial promise of work that might, over time, lead somewhere meaningful. And sometimes, I reminded myself, that's all a first session can truly achieve: the willingness to show up, to stay, and to take the next step when the world still feels uncertain. Sometimes the beginning is all we have.

The echoes of her presence lingered—the tension in her shoulders, the defiance in her glance, the small, almost imperceptible ways she had tested the space even as she sat. I sank back into my chair and opened her intake packet, letting the words and numbers settle around me. Stimulants were her primary substances of choice, alongside cannabis and alcohol at times. This led to functional impairments in housing and employment, repeated risk exposure, fractured family relationships—these were the facts she had shared, patterns as familiar as they are heartbreaking in this work, etched into the stories of those who've sat where she did, carrying similar weights. Her file read like so many before it, yet her presence had already made it unmistakably her own.

Her medical and psychiatric history was extensive: respiratory issues, though she still smoked; stable on medication for now, but with a history of inconsistent adherence; noted allergies; diagnoses including mood and psychotic disorders; and a long history of self-harm and suicidal ideation. Layers of trauma threaded through her life, emergency visits marked recent years, and her existence had balanced on frail edges for years.

In her session, she had only offered fragments of fact—a clinical overview of her history, without the personal narrative or the weight of what these experiences meant to her. Even so, her decision to remain in the chair and engage despite resistance hinted at the first threads of willingness. The session hadn't produced dramatic breakthroughs, but it had yielded something equally crucial: insight, observation, and a tentative foundation of trust. Every gesture, every pause, every flicker across her face became a piece of a puzzle that I could begin to understand and work with.

As I sifted through the intake notes, I reflected on the rhythm of our interaction—the careful pacing, the measured questions, the small moments where she allowed a connection. These subtle indicators weren't just signs of resistance; they were also indicators of potential engagement. I realized that, while she was still firmly in the preparation stage of change, there was a spark of hope: she had chosen to show up, to participate in the assessment, and to stay present even as she fiercely guarded herself. That recognition alone was significant—it told me there was a path forward, even if the journey would be long and cautious.

I began organizing my reflections into a structured framework, noting both the severity of her challenges and the opportunities the session had revealed. Her history, behaviors, and tentative engagement became the roadmap for the next steps. It wasn't about forcing insight or controlling outcomes; it was about accurately capturing the session, understanding the foundation she was willing to allow, and preparing for the careful, patient work ahead. For all the chaos her life reflected, this moment—this small act of staying and listening—was a first step toward something that might one day resemble hope—a fragile step, but one that carried more weight than she likely realized.

A week later, I found myself dialing Raven's number, the phone heavy in my hand as if it carried the weight of the work ahead. Each ring seemed to stretch longer than it should, filling the space of my office with a slight tension I could feel in my chest. When she answered, her voice carried the same guarded tone I remembered from our first encounter—cautious, wary, measured—but beneath it, there was something else, just a flicker: recognition, a trace of the connection we had begun to build.

I spoke slowly and carefully, reminding her of our previous meeting and the reason for my call. I invited her back to the office for her first therapy session, keeping my words simple, patient, and without expectation. There was a pause on her end, just long enough to make me feel the weight of her consideration, the careful deliberation that had become part of how she navigated the world. Then she agreed, softly, almost reluctantly—but clearly. That single word was enough to mark a modest milestone: a willingness to engage, to take one more step toward the work ahead. Sometimes the smallest yes can reshape the entire arc of a therapeutic journey.

I lingered on the line just a moment longer, giving her space to process, to absorb the invitation, and to make it hers. When I hung up, a sense of cautious optimism settled over me. The choice she had made, however small or tentative, was significant. It wasn't a declaration, not a breakthrough, but it was the continuation of a thread we had begun to weave—a thin line of trust that could be strengthened, slowly, session by session. It felt like holding a needle and thread and hoping to see the tapestry grow one stitch at a time.

As I put the phone down, I allowed myself a moment to reflect on what that agreement meant: she had chosen to return, to enable the process to unfold, and to meet me halfway in the work. The next session was still unknown, still uncertain, but in that quiet, deliberate yes, I could already see the faintest outline of possibility. It was a reminder that patience, presence, and unwavering attention were the tools that would guide us forward, one careful step at a time.

The day of Raven's first therapy session arrived, and I felt a mixture of nerves and uncontrollable excitement coiled throughout my body. I could feel it, every pulse, but I also reminded myself to stay mindful, to ground in the moment, to bring the calm presence I had promised her in our first meeting. The office smelled faintly of coffee and cleaning solution, the usual quiet punctuated by the ticking of the wall clock. I glanced at her file one last time, then exhaled slowly, letting the anticipation settle into a steady rhythm.

When she walked in, she carried the same willful, guarded energy I had come to expect. Her hair was tangled, hanging unevenly over her shoulders, her clothes wrinkled and mismatched, her shoes scuffed as if barely noticed. Arms crossed, eyes wary, posture rigid, she sat across from me with the faintest trace of defiance etched into every movement. Her presence was a challenge and an invitation at the same time: a test of patience, of skill, of whether I could truly meet her where she was. I greeted her calmly, inviting her to take a seat and make herself comfortable, though I knew "comfortable" was not a word she would claim just yet.

The session began slowly, deliberately. She answered questions with clipped sentences, often deflecting, sometimes shifting the topic entirely. Her resistance was palpable, but I leaned into it, offering unconditional positive regard and using a technique I had honed over the years—rolling with resistance. Instead of pushing, I mirrored, reflected, and acknowledged her hesitations, letting her feel seen without judgment. Gradually, I noticed small shifts: a softened shoulder, a hand uncrossing, a brief glance that met mine for longer than before, a loose strand of hair falling across her face as she finally adjusted her posture. These were small, but in sessions like this, they speak loudest.

After what felt like a long, careful stretch of observation and measured dialogue, a crack appeared in her armor. I asked about her relationships, and she hesitated, then began talking—tentatively at first—about her partner. As she described the dynamic, the behaviors became clear: frequent arguments, verbal manipulation, subtle controlling tendencies, emotional highs and lows that left her exhausted and anxious. For each point she raised, I reflected it back to her nonjudgmentally, highlighting patterns without blame and helping her see the dynamics without internalizing shame. I stayed present, listening deeply, guiding gently, and allowing her to narrate her own story without feeling pressured.

By the end of the session, the shift was undeniable. Raven's voice had softened, her posture loosened, the guarded edges that had defined her entrance were now slightly rounded, and the disheveled, unkempt aspects of her appearance somehow seemed less like armor and more like traces of her daily battles. As she stood to leave, she turned toward me and, almost casually, said, "You're easy to talk to." I froze for a moment, dumbfounded—not because I hadn't been confident in my approach, but because hearing it from her, in her guarded, cautious tone, carried a weight I hadn't expected. For someone who lived behind walls, even those four simple words felt like a rare offering of appreciation.

She left the office with her usual deliberate movements, hair falling loosely over her face, clothes shifting as she moved, but something had changed—slightly, quietly, in ways that could only be measured over time. I sat back in my chair, exhaling slowly, absorbing the significance of the moment. It wasn't a victory, not yet. But it was enough to know that the thread we had begun to weave in the intake session was holding, however delicately—a filament I've watched strengthen in the hands of others, session by shadowed session. And as I watched the door close behind her, I realized that this was only the beginning.

As she left the office, I sat back in my chair, reflecting. Her words— "You're easy to talk to"—echoed in my mind, a tiny beacon amid all the resistance and guardedness. Nothing had been resolved; nothing had been fixed. Yet something had shifted. The thread we had begun to weave was holding, if only barely, and it was enough to make me lean forward in anticipation rather than retreat.

I glanced at her empty chair, the small indents in the cushion where she had sat, and realized that the story wasn't over. It had only begun. How far she would allow me to follow, how much she would let herself be seen, how long the work would take—these questions hung in the air, unanswered. I didn't know if the next session would bring breakthroughs, breakdowns, or more guarded silence. All I knew was that I would be there, waiting, ready to meet her wherever she chose to show up. Presence, after all, is its own quiet promise.

The clock ticked steadily, unbothered by my thoughts, marking time that felt both infinite and fleeting. Outside, life moved on, but in that office, a possibility had been planted. And for the first time, I felt it—the faint, persistent pulse of hope, unclaimed but unmistakable, and in my heart, I knew she would be back.

CHAPTER 6 - THE TALE OF ALEX

Recovery in Motion

"Sometimes progress looks like ordinary life finally becoming sustainable."

"Recovery is rarely a dramatic leap; more often, it's a quiet momentum built in small, consistent steps."

THE TALE OF ALEX

Recovery in Motion

I first met Alex on a chilly Tuesday morning. The sun hadn't yet broken through the clouds. The sky was gray, like a thick blanket pressing down on the day, heavy with anticipation. He shuffled into the office like someone who had carried the weight of the world on his shoulders for far too long. His coat draped loosely over his frame, edges worn from countless journeys. His bag slumped as if burdened with more than just essentials. Each step he took seemed measured, as if the floor itself might betray him. Even before he spoke, I could see it—the way he moved, the way his gaze scanned the edges of the space, the way he assessed the room like a traveler on unfamiliar ground. He was cautious, measured, and calculating, a strategist even in silence.

I'd heard bits about him from other counselors—stories that painted him as insightful, resilient, and fiercely independent. Whispers of complex emotional patterns lingered in their notes, unexplored and unnamed. Many who worked with him in the past said he was favorable. Favorable, yes, but edged with caution. They all said he didn't trust easily. It was the kind of reputation that followed him like a shadow, hinting at both brilliance and heartbreak. I invited him back to my office. As he entered the room, he stood there, hesitant, as if each decision—whether to sit or leave—carried immense weight, like a crossroad with unseen consequences, every choice echoing with past betrayals.

I had a hunch that the counselors' warnings were understatements. This caution wasn't casual—it was armor, forged in fires I'd seen, tempering the resolve of so many before him, each plate a story of survival's sharp edge. Many clients arrive on guard, ready to defend themselves, believing their chainmail will provide protection. But I am a skilled and considerate observer; it was only a matter of time before I would find a weak link in his protective suit. And yet, I knew it would require patience—a gentle persistence rather than any abrupt force. From the looks of it, his armor had been hammered into place a long time ago, constricting his movement and his very ability to breathe. It would be my job to help loosen the metal plates that held him so tightly.

Alex had every reason not to trust anyone in the program. His last counselor had betrayed him in the worst way possible: breaching a deeply personal confidence in the group, exposing a hidden part of his identity. He did not know that I knew. I could understand how he didn't just feel exposed; he felt humiliated and attacked in a place that should have been a safe haven. The memory was a phantom limb, invisible but present, reminding him that safety was never guaranteed. The ripple of that moment carried through the months that followed, leaving him cautious, guarded, and skeptical of the very system meant to help him. He carried the memory like a battle scar, still tender, still aching, and unamended, a wound that resisted closure.

And yet, here he was. Back. Seeking help for his drug use—the kind I'd seen etched in so many faces across my years in this work, each carrying their quiet storms. That told me something important: despite the walls, despite the pain, there was a spark of hope—a desire to find freedom. There was something stubborn about that hope, like a single candle flickering in a hurricane, refusing to die. And that stubborn light—it drew me in, quietly demanding that I meet him with equal resolve, to stand as steady as the flame itself.

There was a tension in the air, subtle yet tangible, like static before a storm. I could feel the weight of his caution pressing against the walls of the room, a pressure that demanded respect. And yet, I also sensed a restlessness within him, a longing for something he could not yet name. A hunger that flickered beneath the armor.

Alex finally sat down in the chair, arms folded, gaze scanning the edges of the space as if the walls themselves were going to judge him. He spoke slowly at first, measuring each word, selective and cautious, like stepping on thin ice, trying to cross a frozen pond. I could tell he was experienced with this part of the therapeutic process—a veteran of conversations that often felt more like battles than healing.

With a deep and heavy inhale and exhale, he spoke. "What do you want to know?" he asked, his tone almost baiting, as if daring me to judge him, testing whether I would wound or withstand.

Little did he know that I was also experienced with this process?

"Only what you want me to know," I said, keeping my voice calm, "only what you are comfortable sharing."

There was a pause as we looked at each other. A stalemate. To this day, I believe he recognized my skill as a therapist, and he knew I recognized his experience as a seeker of healing. I broke the silence first.

"Trust takes a long time to build," I told him. "I don't expect you to tell me your entire life story on day one. In fact, I'd be worried if you did." A slight smile tugged at the corner of his mouth, a hint that he was amused. I continued.

"I'd like to know about your past experiences with counselors and therapists. Things you liked, things you didn't. Ways in which you were helped, and ways in which things weren't so helpful."

He told me about counselors who had tried too hard to fix him, therapists who had dismissed him, treatment methods that he enjoyed, and others he didn't. He did not mention that specific breach of trust, nor did I let on that I knew one of his most painful moments as a client. It would take him months to work up the courage to tell me that story—months of circling the wound before daring to expose it.

I listened. More than that, I watched. The subtle tensing in his jaw when he remembered the painful experiences. The way his hands tightened around the armrests when he discussed past mistakes and pain caused by professionals. I stored it all silently in the forefront of my mind, noting the methods I would need to gently reach him. I didn't offer judgment or advice yet—I couldn't. My job was to observe, to understand, and to meet him where he was, no matter how far from trust that place might be. It was an exercise in patience, an unspoken promise to honor his readiness and autonomy. If I could subtly nudge him in the right direction, I might help him feel heard and validated, and offer him a sense of freedom. I might help him breathe before he walks out of here, to leave lighter than he arrived.

Even as he spoke, I began noticing patterns, little rhythms in his story: moments when he felt safe, moments when he pulled away, phrases he repeated when frustrated. These patterns were clues, breadcrumbs that would help me build a bridge to him.

I noticed his hesitation when he talked about certain counselors—how his tone would change when describing someone who had tried to control him, or who had used fear as leverage to enhance counselor-driven treatment. He spoke about counselors who had told him that if he didn't stop using, he would die— a stark warning I'd heard echoed in too many rooms, a chorus of fear that silenced more than it saved—insisting that he withdraw and "get his life right." That was a recurring theme he experienced with every counselor. The words had been blunt, almost cruel, stripped of empathy. Alex had remembered sitting there, paralyzed by the weight of those ultimatums, feeling cornered by a system that was supposed to help, not to judge.

"It was like they didn't see me," he said softly, almost to himself. "All they wanted was for me to comply. They didn't care how I got there, just that I went their way."

In that moment, I understood: for Alex, recovery could not be forced. It could not be dictated or scheduled, and he could not be convinced. Any attempt to impose change on him would only reinforce the walls he had spent years building. He would need freedom, autonomy, and the knowledge that the choice was his—and his alone, a path he must claim, not inherit.

I had to check my emotions. I began to feel angry. I saw patterns among counselors who, for various reasons, appeared overly connected to their clients. Maybe they themselves feared for the client's well-being—a real fear, given that a seeker could be in the office one week and lost the next. Counselors who forget to check their own emotions before engaging clients often lose objectivity and risk ending up doing the very opposite of what they intend, offering control instead of care.

I also reflected on the paradox of his strength—how survival had hardened him, yet that same strength carried fragility. It was a balance: too much pressure and the walls would hold firm; too little, and he might slip away from engagement entirely. Every word, every pause, every glance mattered.

I lingered with Alex beyond the usual first-session bounds. My afternoon was open, and I needed the time. I asked him about his life history. I let him speak, story after story, memory after memory, each tale revealing a little more of the man behind the armor. I paid attention to the subtle cues—his hands, his eyes, the way his voice trembled at some moments and hardened at others. I weighed his likes, dislikes, preferences, and patterns in my mind, building a mental map that would guide our work together. I realized that every pause, every subtle inflection, every glance was as much a message as the words themselves, silent signals that spoke louder than speech.

It struck me how much human connection is unspoken—how much trust is built not in what is said, but in the acknowledgment of presence. To truly meet Alex, I had to inhabit the spaces between his words, honor the hesitations, and allow silence to breathe alongside conversation.

When he reached a place where it looked like there was nothing else for him to say, I finally responded.

A simple statement that seemed to take Alex completely off guard—so much so that he had me repeat it. I looked him in the eye and said,

"Alex, after hearing your story and understanding the way you use substances, a rhythm I've traced in countless others who've walked through these doors, each variation a thread in the same unraveling tapestry, I am convinced that you are not ready for withdrawal management or residential treatment."

He blinked; shock held him in disbelief. There was a pause, heavy with a mix of relief and confusion. No one had ever said that to him before—not quite like that. There was no lecture, no judgment, no rush to force him into a process he wasn't ready for. Just recognition. It was an acknowledgment of where he truly stood, not where anyone else thought he should.

Alex leaned back, his posture slightly slumped, but his eyes sharp, curious. Then he asked a valid question:

"Are you worried I'm going to lose myself to an overdose—the shadow that has haunted so many I've held space for, a specter we name but cannot always outrun?"

I nodded. "Yes," I said, keeping my voice calm and measured. "It's always a possibility, and it would be unfortunate. But what you've described about your using patterns, the way you've learned to manage your own harm, tempers that worry. I know you understand the risk of death, and yet you continue to use. However, that should not stop us from meeting, though."

Alex stared at me for a long moment, processing. There was no judgment in my words, no alarm—just recognition of reality and a willingness to sit with it. For someone like him, who had spent years being treated like a problem to be solved, not a person to be understood—and I'd seen that dismissal carve deeper wounds in so many before—that was rare.

We continued for a few more minutes, carefully winding down the session. As I began to gather my notes, Alex asked another question, quieter this time, almost hesitant:

"Do you know when I'll be ready for withdrawal? For residential treatment?"

I looked at him, meeting his gaze. There was no crystal ball, no instant answer, and I wasn't going to offer false certainty.

"I won't," I said slowly. "But you will. One day in the future, you'll wake up in the morning with a sense of motivation, and you'll call me. You'll know. You'll know when you're ready for that part of the treatment. And until then, we work with what we have. We meet where you are, not where anyone thinks you should be."

He leaned back, letting out a breath he hadn't realized he was holding. There was no breakthrough, no instant trust, no resolution. Just the simplest understanding that this was his path, on his terms, and I would be there to walk beside him when he was ready.

That moment stayed with me long after the session ended. It wasn't dramatic, and there were no grand epiphanies. But in its simplicity, in the patience it demanded, it carried a subtle power—the kind that doesn't push change but honors it when it comes. For Alex, and for any seeker who had been let down too many times before, that mattered more than anything else I could offer.

As I left the room that morning, I thought about the lessons hidden in that first encounter: patience, respect, and the therapeutic art of meeting someone exactly where they are. Recovery isn't a race. It isn't a checklist or a timeline. It's a process—sometimes slow, sometimes painful, sometimes invisible, sometimes shadowed by peril—built on small steps, on earned trust, and on the simple understanding that the person sitting across from you is the expert on their own readiness. And sometimes, the smallest acts—the act of listening, the act of waiting, the act of acknowledging—can be more transformative than any grand gesture.

And I realized, too, that my work with Alex was not about rushing or controlling, but about cultivating patience within myself. Sometimes the most challenging part of therapy is learning to wait for trust to emerge, to honor the invisible currents of a person's readiness, and to recognize that even the slightest flicker of hope can illuminate the darkest spaces, a fragile light that teaches both seeker and guide to believe again.

CHAPTER 7 - THE TALE OF JORDAN

Perceptions of Reality

"Perception is fragile, and reality is often subjective — two people can sit in the same room and live entirely different truths."

"Even the unfinished stories leave an imprint — a reminder of the humility required to witness someone's life unfold."

THE TALE OF JORDAN

Perceptions of Reality

One of the advantages of working in an office with deep roots in the community and a team that stays year after year is the wisdom you gain from your colleagues. I remember that morning vividly. I was walking down the hallway when our office administrator called me over, her tone carrying that quiet urgency that makes you stop in your tracks. "J, we need to talk about an intake I just set you up with," she said.

I followed her into her office without hesitation, curious. She closed the door, sat down, and leaned back in her chair slightly. With a deep sigh, she began to talk about Jordan—a client whose story, I quickly realized, was going to challenge not just my understanding of him, but my own perception of reality, the assumptions I carried, and the way I thought about human behavior in the therapeutic space. Before I even had a chance to meet Jordan, it seemed like everyone wanted to give me their two cents.

The office manager shared her observations, the clinical supervisor provided her notes, and some of the other counselors even stopped by to offer their thoughts. I could feel the undercurrent of concern, but also care—everyone had his best interest at heart. They weren't warning me off him in a dismissive way; they were giving context, sharing nuances, and emphasizing the patterns they had seen over time. Words like complex mental health patterns, episodes of altered perception, unmanaged challenges, and stimulant use came up frequently, each comment layering onto the picture they were trying to paint. Each observation felt like a fragment of a larger story, a map I would have to navigate carefully.

These shared insights weren't about one man alone; they were threads from a tapestry of lives I'd seen unfold—patterns that repeated across many intakes, each client a variation on resilience's quiet fray, indistinguishable in their shared humanity. Yet, even with all the information, there was a sense of collaboration rather than warning—everyone just wanted to make sure I was set up to help Jordan as best I could. By the time I finally met him, I was carrying their insights and perspectives, a patchwork of observations, assumptions, and professional instincts.

I couldn't help but imagine what Jordan would look like. In my mind, Jordan had already taken shape: disheveled, unkempt, ungrounded, disoriented—the kind of client who might be a challenge to have a conversation with. I braced myself for the possible unpredictability I had been warned about. But when I finally met him, none of that was the case. He walked in with a calm presence, made eye contact, and spoke with clarity and conviction that forced me to confront the assumptions I had carried in my mind. Jordan didn't fit the picture I had painted for myself based on the office's notes and warnings. He reminded me, almost immediately, that my perception of someone's reality is never the full story.

Jordan began to tell his story, and at first, it was strikingly coherent. He spoke of a life that had once been structured and purposeful. He had once navigated a structured life with family commitments and a demanding service role—a path that demanded discipline, resilience, and dedication. Slowly, though, the story shifted. Substance use crept into his life, initially as a way to cope, to manage stress, to feel alive.

Over time, it consumed him, eroding relationships, leading to strained connections, entanglements with the system, and eventually periods of instability. As he spoke, each detail was delivered with conviction, a thread of clarity running through the chaos of his past. It was a narrative that made sense, linear in its progression, yet beneath the surface, I sensed complexities that weren't immediately visible, waiting for me to notice. There was a subtle tension in the air, a sense that more lurked in the spaces between his words. As Jordan's story continued, the shadowed path of substance challenges and instability unfolded, held together only by the meagre support of state and county-funded programs.

Up to this point, his narrative had been linear, almost textbook in its tragic clarity. But slowly, that structure began to fray. Jordan started weaving in stories of people, events, and hidden forces so vivid they seemed to hover between fact and imagination—tales involving elusive threats from the wild, massive presences you might expect to find in untamed lands, and connections that twisted through neighborhoods, agencies, and chance encounters. He spoke with such conviction, such certainty, that for a moment I questioned what was real and what was constructed.

His narrative challenged my assumptions, reminding me that reality, at least the reality of the person sitting across from you, is never as simple or stable as it appears—a truth I'd gleaned from labyrinths of perception in so many sessions before, where conviction and chaos danced in equal measure, a rhythm echoed in the untold stories of those who've sat in similar silences before. Each new layer of his story felt like a door opening into a world I was not fully prepared to enter. To make matters even more complicated, Jordan's ability to recall realistic events added another layer of tension to his story.

He spoke with vivid detail about an incident in his living space—an encounter with a massive, unseen danger that forced him to flee. According to him, he ran down the stairs, out into the street, and collided with authorities. He insisted he had been protecting them after accidentally knocking one over, but in his account, that encounter led to his entanglement with the system. Jordan's voice carried a certainty that made it difficult to dismiss, and he claimed he demanded footage to prove his side of the story. The conviction in his tone made me pause, a reminder that lived experience is filtered through perception rather than objectivity.

As he recounted it, I found myself navigating the space between listening with empathy and trying to maintain a grasp on what felt plausible—a balance that challenged every assumption I had about reality, perception, and the way a story can be told. As Jordan spoke, I felt the familiar tug of doubt and curiosity pulling at my mind. Every detail was delivered with such conviction that it demanded acknowledgment, yet some of it pressed against the edges of plausibility. I had to remind myself to stay grounded—to listen without judgment and to honor his experience, even as it challenged my own sense of reality. His story forced me to confront the assumptions I carried: about coherence, about cause and effect, about what a "real" account of events should look like.

In that room, with Jordan sitting across from me, I realized that the therapeutic process wasn't just about guiding him—it was about holding a space where his reality, however fragmented or fantastical it seemed, could exist alongside mine without collapse. It was a space that needed patience, quiet observation, and unwavering respect for his lived experience. It's a lesson drilled into you in school, repeated in supervision, and reinforced by experience: never argue with someone about their episodes of altered perception. To them, those moments are as real as the air in the room, as tangible as the chair they're sitting in. You can't win, and trying only erodes trust. With Jordan, that truth became immediate and unavoidable.

Every word he spoke about the unseen dangers, the authorities, the hidden forces—it was all real to him, and my role wasn't to dispute it. My job was to witness, to contain, and to find a path forward that honored his reality while keeping both him and the therapeutic space intact. I reminded myself that judgment had no place here; only presence and observation mattered. Sitting there with Jordan, I had to check my own reactions constantly. The stories he told were vivid, full of danger and intrigue, but my role wasn't to correct him or challenge the details—it was to listen, to validate his experience, and to hold the space steady.

I focused on his feelings: the fear, the isolation, the frustration that threaded through every tale. Each time he insisted on the truth of what he had seen, I acknowledged it without judgment, letting him feel heard while quietly mapping the contours of his reality. It was a dance of patience and restraint, one that required me to hold my own sense of reality lightly while fully engaging with his. Every subtle shift in tone, every pause, was a signal I could follow to navigate the next step. In that room, the therapeutic work wasn't about proving right or wrong—it was about building trust and connection in a world where clarity and chaos coexisted side by side. As I listened, I started considering how to guide him toward a path that could truly benefit him. It wasn't about correcting his reality or forcing him to see things my way—it was about finding the threads in his story that could be used as anchors. Moments of clarity, patterns in his life before substance challenges, the structure he once maintained in family and service life—all of it could become points to build from.

My goal became finding a foothold, a way to guide him gently toward safety and stability without dismissing the truths he held in his own mind. In that moment, I realized that therapy with Jordan wouldn't be linear; it would require patience, creativity, and a careful mapping of his reality as he experienced it. Listening closely, I began to notice the patterns in Jordan's life that offered real insight. Despite everything—the substance challenges, the broken connections, the instability—he had managed to achieve periods of sobriety before. There was proof in the past that he was capable of structure and resilience, even if it had been fleeting.

It wasn't luck or coincidence; it had been a combination of structured support, guidance, and programs like support groups, along with resources through veteran services. He had built bridges to others who shared the echoes of service life and the unique challenges of reintegration. These were tangible successes, evidence that he could navigate stability when given the right tools and guidance. Recognizing this wasn't just about hope—it was about strategy.

If he had found a way before, there was a path forward again.

My job became identifying how to connect him with those same supports while respecting his current reality, building a bridge between what he had done in the past and what he could do now. As I considered Jordan's story and the glimpses of success he had achieved in the past, it became clear that a solution-focused approach might serve him best. This wasn't about dissecting every altered moment or debating the veracity of his experiences—it was about providing concrete steps that could improve his day-to-day life, build stability, and reinforce the strengths he already possessed.

By focusing on what worked for him before—guidance, structured programs, support gatherings, veteran resources—we could create a practical, forward-looking plan that honored his reality while giving him tools to navigate it more safely, drawing from the successes I'd witnessed in others who'd navigated similar shadows, where small anchors held against the tide, lessons drawn not from one path but from the collective drift of many unseen journeys. It was subtle work, the kind that required patience, respect, and careful guidance, but it offered a tangible pathway in a situation that otherwise felt unpredictable and overwhelming.

By the end of our first session, I felt we had begun to shape a plan—a framework that Jordan could start implementing right away. We identified several concrete steps: first, stabilizing his supports to establish a foundation for clarity and consistency; second, considering entry into structured living options that could provide routine and safety; and third, reconnecting with veteran resources to access the guidance he had relied on in the past. Each step was deliberate, measurable, and aligned with his lived experience.

Each step was grounded in his own history of success, and for the first time in our time together, there was a sense of direction. Jordan seemed to recognize it too—the plan wasn't a prescription imposed on him, but a set of achievable actions he could take, one by one, to regain stability and control in his life. In addition to stabilizing on his supports, Jordan agreed to attend weekly one-on-one sessions, alongside regular group gatherings.

The combination offered both individualized attention and the opportunity to gain experience from peers—an environment where he could process his experiences, practice coping strategies, and begin to rebuild trust. The group setting, in particular, provided a mirror of sorts, reflecting both challenges and progress in real time. Together, these sessions created a rhythm, a steady anchor that could reinforce the other steps in his plan, and for Jordan, it was another piece of the structure that might help him regain control over his life. It was a fragile but promising scaffold, one that could support growth if nurtured consistently.

For the next few weeks, it seemed as though we had found a solution. Jordan consistently engaged with his support system, lived in transitional housing that provided structure and safety, and attended gatherings with fellow service peers. He had reconnected with veteran resources, accessing guidance that had supported him in the past, and he was reliably showing up for both his one-on-one sessions and group meetings at the therapy office. There was a tentative steadiness in his routine, a slow building rhythm that felt fragile yet promising.

There was a rhythm to his life again, a sense of momentum that hadn't been present for years. I found myself quietly celebrating the small victories with him—watching him take the steps that, on paper, were simple but in reality required immense courage and effort. And yet, even in those first weeks of growing stability, some moments reminded me how slow progress can be. A missed call from the transitional staff here, a brief absence from a gathering there—small cracks that hinted at the difficulty of maintaining engagement when a person's life has been as chaotic as Jordan's.

I reminded myself that recovery is rarely linear; even seemingly minor disruptions can cascade into larger setbacks if not carefully supported. Then, slowly, it began to feel like everything we had built was slipping away. Jordan stopped coming to his meetings. He ceased staying in contact with the therapeutic staff and would not engage in any of the services that had been so carefully mapped out. The silence was heavy, carrying with it the echo of uncertainty and unfulfilled potential.

Weeks later, he was ultimately found in a distant urban shadow, deeply immersed in his patterns of escape. The stability we had worked to create seemed fragile, almost illusory, and I was forced to confront the reality that progress in someone's life—especially one so tangled with substance challenges and layered experiences—was never guaranteed, no matter how clear the path or how motivated the person appeared to be. It was a sobering reminder of the limits of even the most attentive guidance.

Sitting with the weight of Jordan's relapse, I had to reflect on what had gone wrong—and what could be done next. It wasn't a failure of strategy, nor a lack of effort on his part; it was a reminder that recovery isn't linear, and that setbacks are part of the process—a setback not unlike those that had rippled through the lives of countless seekers before him, teaching me that proper accompaniment means holding space for the unseen currents that bind all such returns to the edge.

I thought about the support that had worked before, the moments of clarity he had experienced, and how to reconnect him with those foundations without judgment or pressure. The challenge was to rebuild trust, reestablish structure, and help him see a pathway forward that felt achievable, even after such a significant setback. In that moment's reflection, I reminded myself that therapy is as much about patience and persistence as it is about planning, and that the work isn't over simply because a step back has occurred.

Of course, all of these plans and reflections were contingent on one critical factor: Jordan's willingness to engage. Without his participation, even the most carefully crafted strategies amounted to nothing more than ideas on paper. I had to face the uncomfortable truth that recovery requires collaboration; it cannot be imposed. If he chose not to show up, not to connect, not to take even the smallest steps toward stability, then progress might never happen. That truth, though difficult, underscored the delicate balance of agency and support that defines therapeutic work.

That reality weighed heavily—it was a reminder that, ultimately, the path forward depended as much on his choices as on any guidance I could offer. Ultimately, Jordan never returned. After repeated attempts to reach and re-engage him in services, he was formally discharged. Even now, I still see his name pop up in our system from time to time—intakes scheduled, hopeful notes left, only for him not to show.

Each time, there's a flicker of hope, a quiet wish that he might finally take that step, and a reminder of the reality we often face in this work: sometimes, despite the best efforts, the timing isn't right. The opportunity to walk alongside someone doesn't always come when we want it to, and the outcomes are never guaranteed. Jordan's story left me with a quiet, lingering set of lessons.

I was reminded that perception is fragile, that reality is often subjective, and that a client's conviction in their own story can challenge even the most experienced clinician. I learned that progress is never linear, and that patience, persistence, and empathy are as critical as any plan or intervention. Most importantly, I was reminded that our role is to hold space—to provide guidance, support, and structure—while recognizing that ultimately, the client must choose when and how to step onto the path of change. This is the paradox of care: to guide without controlling, to wait without giving up.

Jordan may not have returned, but the experience reinforced for me the delicate balance of trust, hope, and acceptance that defines this work, and the humility required to witness someone's life unfold, whether or not we are there for every step. Even months later, reflecting on Jordan's case, I carry the memory of both his clarity and his chaos. His presence reminds me to approach each new client with curiosity, to suspend judgment, and to honor the complexity of lived experience. It is a reminder that every story, no matter how unfinished, leaves a mark.

Jordan's narrative, with its strange twists and moments of coherence, continues to influence the way I listen, plan, and hold space for those whose realities stretch the limits of my own understanding. In the end, the work is not about control—it is about accompaniment. It is about recognizing that sometimes the most profound impact we can have is simply being present, ready to guide, to watch, and to wait until the client chooses to walk the path themselves. Jordan's case continues to echo in my practice, shaping the way I approach every client who walks through the door.

He reminded me that therapy isn't about imposing reality, it's about meeting someone where they are—sometimes in spaces that feel impossible to navigate, sometimes in worlds that challenge everything I think I know. I learned to honor the tension between what is real to me and what is real to them, and to hold that space with patience rather than urgency. Jordan taught me that progress isn't always visible, that success isn't always measured in attendance or adherence to a plan, and that the simple act of showing up—of waiting, listening, and witnessing—is itself a form of care. It is a quiet, persistent form of presence that can ripple far beyond the session.

In many ways, every client since Jordan carries a trace of that lesson, weaving in the faint echoes of those who'd come before, each adding to the art of presence I carry forward. I find myself more attentive to the subtleties, the small threads of stability hidden in chaos, and more willing to let the process unfold at its own pace. Therapy, I've come to understand, is less about control and more about accompaniment—an art of presence, of trust, and of humility.

Jordan didn't need me to fix his reality; he needed me to hold it alongside mine without judgment, to offer guidance when he was ready, and to stay prepared, no matter how long the waiting might take. And in holding that space for him, I have learned to hold it for every client who will follow, carrying forward the quiet, unassuming power of patience, trust, and unwavering presence. It is a lesson that lingers, shaping each decision and every moment of listening in the work that comes after.

CHAPTER 8 - THE TALE OF RILEY

Metaphors

"Clients speak in storms, whispers, riddles, and silence — and all of it is language."

"A therapist learns to listen for the tremor beneath words — the truth hiding between breaths."

THE TALE OF RILEY

Metaphors

Clients speak in many languages, and not all of them use words the way we expect. In therapy, language is more than communication—it is armor, confession, and sometimes the only form of control a person feels they have left. Some clients speak in storms, letting loose whirlwinds of memory and pain as if reliving everything for the first time. The air itself seems charged with the echoes of their inner turbulence. So much pours into the room that it feels less like conversation and more like walking through the aftermath—searching for what still aches and what might finally heal.

Others whisper, as if giving voice to their story might break something inside. Their words come out like riddles, and the therapist becomes a detective, following clues in what is said and what is left unsaid. Some fill the silence with chatter to keep it at bay. Others let silence speak—heavy, deliberate, like the hush before everything changes. In these moments, the room itself becomes a participant, holding the weight of what is shared and what remains unspoken.

A therapist learns to listen for the tremor beneath words spoken, the truth hiding between breaths. Some lessons come from books and training; most come from sitting in rooms while stories spill. You have to grow comfortable with pauses, patient enough to let meaning rise slowly, yet ready to catch the truths that flood out all at once. Over time, you learn to read the hesitations, the half-finished thoughts, the tiny glimmers that carry whole worlds inside them. Every gesture, every shift in posture, every flicker of expression becomes a piece of the story.

But Riley spoke a language that was difficult to understand—one built entirely from pictures, symbols, and scenes so vivid they felt like stepping into another world. He came to therapy exhausted with a world that never seemed to understand him. Jobs slipped away, relationships faded, and he kept falling into old habits that quieted the noise for a little while. Beneath the anger and the weariness, though, I could feel something else: a deep longing to belong, to feel truly seen, to believe something better was still possible. There was a restlessness in him, a yearning that reached beyond his struggles, hinting at the resilience he had yet to fully claim. It was a quiet insistence that he was still seeking something beyond mere survival.

Our first several sessions were slow and quiet. My usual questions felt clumsy, like knocking on a door that wouldn't open. Words felt inadequate, and my familiar tools—questions, reflections, gentle nudges—felt blunt and distant against the shape of his inner world. In the middle of that silence, a small thread of hope appeared. I reminded myself—and him—that staying present, curious, and patient could still build a bridge, even if it took a long time.

His way of talking was layered, full of hints at feelings he couldn't—or wouldn't—say directly. Sometimes his sentences felt scattered, almost dreamlike, like pieces of colored glass on the floor. Yet there were no hallucinations, no fixed false beliefs, no flatness of emotion—nothing that pointed to the usual patterns we're taught to recognize. His symbolic way of speaking wasn't illness; it was simply the only path his mind still trusted.

I kept going back over my notes, trying to understand what lay behind the images. Nothing obvious stood out—no recent crisis, no clear label. Yet something kept tugging at me, like a memory I couldn't quite place. Riley stayed with me long after sessions ended. His situation, his language, gnawed at the edges of my thoughts—small, relentless, impossible to ignore. There was something eerily familiar about his struggle, a quiet echo that pulled at old knowledge. It was the kind of recognition that hits softly but stays with you. And then, suddenly, it surfaced: Phineas Gage.

Phineas Gage. The name came back like a flare in the dark—a railroad foreman in Vermont, September 13, 1848. A steady, capable man, well-liked, known for his efficiency and good sense. While tamping explosive powder into a hole, the charge went off early. A three-foot-seven-inch iron rod, an inch and a quarter thick, shot upward. It entered beneath his left cheekbone, passed behind his eye, tore through the front part of his brain, and exited through the top of his skull, landing eighty feet away. Everyone expected him to die within minutes. He never even lost consciousness. He lived another twelve years, but the man who walked away from that railroad was not the same man who had arrived that morning. Friends and family said, "Gage is no longer Gage." The injury had rewired his personality, his impulses, his very sense of self. The story lingered in my mind, a historical mirror reflecting the invisible injuries Riley might carry.

I went back to Riley with new eyes, now determined to understand the full weight of what an old injury might have done. When I gently asked whether anything had ever happened to his head—any accident, any blow, any moment

77

that changed everything—he paused for a very long time. The room felt completely still. Then, almost offhand, he said, "Yeah… a long time ago. A bad accident." He described a sudden, violent event from many years earlier that had torn through his skull and left lasting damage the surgeons couldn't fully repair—scar tissue, changes deep inside that no one could see from the outside. He spoke slowly, carefully, pulling the memory up from very far away. There had been noise and then, nothing. When he came back to himself, whole pieces of time were gone—blank spaces where memories should have been.

He said it felt like living in a story with pages ripped out. Sounds were suddenly too sharp, feelings too large, time moved at the wrong speed. He learned to hide the confusion behind anger or escape into habits that dulled his senses. Relationships never lasted because no one could keep up with the storms inside him. Jobs fell apart because focus came and went like the weather changes. The injury was long healed on the outside, but it still shaped every single day.

As our sessions continued, I began to notice something subtle—an emerging rhythm within his language, a pendulum swing between the concrete and the abstract. When asked a direct question, Riley could answer with remarkable clarity. Simple questions—about his sleep, his day, his plans—were met with straightforward, almost clinical precision. But the moment the question delved deeper, touching anything that stirred emotion or meaning, his words began to shift. The air would thicken, and his sentences would turn to symbols, as if emotion demanded a different dialect altogether.

I realized his metaphors weren't a constant—they were a threshold. They appeared when logic alone could no longer contain what he was trying to express. It was as though his mind instinctively reached for art when reason began to tremble. When he felt safe, grounded in the present, he spoke plainly. But when he wandered into uncertainty or pain, he began to talk in landscapes, in storms and broken glass, in forests and fire. His metaphors became a bridge between two languages—the practical world and the one where his old wound still echoed.

From a therapeutic lens, I understood this as both a defense and an adaptation. The metaphor allowed him to explore painful material at a distance, to name what could not be directly spoken without drowning in it. Yet it also created a barrier—a place where he could hide behind imagery when the truth became too close. My task, then, was not to pull him out of the metaphor but to walk beside him within it, to find the real story hidden in its shadows. Over time, I learned to listen for the shift—the moment his voice softened, when description became deflection, when meaning shimmered just beneath the surface of poetry.

It struck me that his healing might not lie in choosing one language over the other, but in learning to move fluidly between them—to speak both with the heart's imagery and the mind's clarity. Riley's metaphors were not a symptom to be corrected but a compass pointing toward the parts of him that still needed to be found.

Over time, patterns began to surface—quiet but unmistakable. Riley could speak clearly and directly when the subject remained simple and anchored in the here and now. Ask him how he slept or what he wanted for the day, and he would respond plainly, almost methodically. But the moment a question brushed against something internal—his fears, his regrets, his sense of self— the clarity dissolved into abstraction. He would drift into metaphor, as if thought itself had slipped through a crack in the floorboards. Each shift was subtle, but the patterns grew more evident with each session, like ripples spreading across a calm pond.

At first, I mistook this for avoidance, a subtle resistance to vulnerability. But the more I listened, the more I understood that his metaphors were not barriers—they were pathways. When his brain reached the limits of linear thought, it sought refuge in imagery. It was not deflection, but translation: a neurological and emotional workaround shaped by both injury and adaptation. He wasn't hiding behind metaphor; he was building through it, creating a language capable of holding what ordinary words could not.

Clinically, it reminded me of how the injured brain sometimes rewires itself—how new pathways form to bypass damaged ones. Psychologically, it mirrored how the mind protects itself when emotion threatens to overwhelm cognition. Riley's metaphors were the intersection of these two truths— neurological compensation meeting emotional defense. He slipped in and out of figurative speech the way some people slip in and out of memory— seamlessly, unconsciously, guided by what the moment demanded.

In session, I learned to recognize the shift. A question would land too close, and his eyes would glaze just slightly, his gaze turning inward. Then came the imagery—the forest, the fire, the storm. Instead of steering him back to plain speech, I began to follow him into those places. "Tell me about the storm," I'd say. "What does it look like today?" And in that symbolic terrain, truths began to emerge that no direct question had ever reached. Small threads of understanding appeared, fragile at first, but strong enough to guide the next step.

Therapeutically, it became clear that Riley's healing would not come from silencing his metaphors. Still, from integrating them—helping him translate the poetry of his pain into language the world could understand. His metaphors weren't confusing; they were his mind's way of reaching toward coherence. And somewhere between the poetry and the plain speech, between the symbol and the self, Riley began to find the rhythm of his own recovery.

In that moment, the parallel became undeniable. Like Gage, Riley's injury had rewritten the architecture of his mind—an unseen hand rearranging the corridors where thought, emotion, and identity once flowed freely. But where Gage's story had been reduced to a lesson in neurology, Riley's was a living testament to what happens when a soul keeps breathing after the map of its mind has been redrawn. His metaphors were not madness; they were translation. They were the language of a brain that had been forced to find new routes through terrain scarred long ago. Every image, every symbol, was a bridge spanning fractured neural pathways.

Suddenly, his storms of speech made sense—the vivid imagery, the strange detours, the fractured poetry of his words. He was not avoiding reality; he was reconstructing it, one image at a time. What I had mistaken for disorganization was, in truth, adaptation—a desperate, ingenious attempt to make meaning where the old neural pathways had gone dark. His metaphors were bridges built from the wreckage of his mind. They were unique but functional, carrying him from confusion to coherence, from isolation toward connection.

I realized then that Riley was not broken—he was rebuilding. The very thing that had once nearly destroyed him had also forced him to become a cartographer of his own inner landscape, redrawing the borders between emotion and reason, memory and meaning. Like Gage, he lived at the intersection of survival and transformation, proof that the mind, even when wounded, can reinvent its own language in order to keep the self-alive. And in that realization, I understood the responsibility and privilege of witnessing such a reconstruction.

In the days that followed, I brought Riley's case into clinical consultation. Around the table sat supervisors and colleagues, each offering a different lens— neurological, psychological, and experiential. Together, we unpacked the patterns, replaying fragments of his speech, his phrasing, and the subtle rhythms that emerged across sessions. The question wasn't whether he could be understood, but how. His language, we agreed, was not a wall but a map—one that required more than one interpreter to read.

The discussion focused on what could be done in the immediate term to support him effectively. We identified the importance of patience—not as passive waiting, but as an active stance of curiosity. Riley's metaphors could not be rushed or decoded in a single sitting; they had to be approached with care, revisited as context emerged. Each image he offered was a fragment of a larger picture, a translation of emotion into symbol. Even within a few sessions, it became clear that understanding him would take time, and our collaborative insight would be essential in that process. The effort demanded vigilance, humility, and attentiveness to every subtle gesture and turn of phrase.

Supervisors emphasized that translation in cases like Riley's rarely happens all at once. It unfolds moment by moment, through repetition, grounding, and trust. My role, they suggested, was not to interpret too quickly but to remain present in the uncertainty—to sit with the metaphor and let its meaning reveal itself gradually. Staff contributed short-term strategies: grounding exercises to steady him when his speech grew abstract, visual prompts to externalize his imagery, and structured check-ins to help connect his symbolism to present reality.

These consultations became vital in shaping the next steps. They reminded me that therapy, especially in complex cases, is never a solitary act but a collaborative one. It takes collective patience and humility to translate a language formed by injury and adaptation. Riley was teaching all of us something quietly profound—that understanding is not immediate, but earned through consistency, curiosity, and the shared effort to see the world through another person's metaphors.

The first few months with Riley were spent learning to speak his language— an exercise in patience, translation, and empathy. Each session felt like stepping into a new dialect, one that used imagery as syntax and emotion as grammar. His metaphors rarely meant what they first appeared to mean. Sometimes they shifted mid-conversation, taking on new shades of meaning depending on the memory or feeling beneath them.

He once said, "My thoughts are like birds that don't know where to land." At first, I assumed he meant distraction or restlessness, but as he elaborated, it became clear he was describing something more profound—a mind in flight, searching for a place of safety that never quite arrived. On another day, he told me, "There's a fire in my head, but it's not burning anything—it just hums." The image seemed chaotic, almost destructive, but to Riley it represented constant motion, the hum of awareness that never let him rest. His metaphors were layered like sediment—each one holding traces of past meanings, stacked upon one another, never entirely replaced. I began to sense that beneath every metaphor lay a pulse of truth, a signal I had to follow carefully.

Those early sessions became less about interpretation and more about exploration. I found that when I tried to restate what I thought he meant in ordinary language, the spark would fade from his eyes. But when I responded in metaphor—when I tried to meet him where he lived symbolically— something shifted. If I said, "Maybe those birds are just tired of flying," he would light up, nodding quickly, eager to expand the image. Other times, he would gently correct me, saying something like, "No, they're not tired—they just don't trust the sky." His corrections weren't defensive; they were clarifications, his way of shaping the shared landscape of understanding between us.

Empathetic listening became the bridge. I learned that reflecting his metaphors back to him wasn't about getting the words right, but about finding resonance—the emotional tone beneath the image. When I rephrased something, and he smiled or leaned forward, I knew I had touched the truth he was trying to express. When he frowned or redirected, it meant I had missed the mark, and the conversation turned into a collaborative act of translation. Slowly, through this back-and-forth rhythm of metaphor and re-metaphor, we began to build trust. Each small connection felt like a stepping stone across a vast, turbulent river, fragile yet sturdy enough to bear our weight.

Those early months weren't about treatment plans or measurable progress; they were about understanding—the kind that takes place quietly, beneath the surface of words. I realized that Riley didn't need me to translate his language into something more clinical or digestible. He needed me to learn it, to speak it with him, and to help him find meaning within it, rather than looking outside for it. And little by little, through this shared effort, his metaphors began to lose some of their loneliness. They became less like riddles and more like bridges—connecting him, at last, to someone willing to listen in his native tongue.

Over the next several months, my sessions with Riley became an immersion course in his personal lexicon. Each phrase, each image, became a clue—a hieroglyph of emotion that, when decoded, revealed the contours of his inner world. I started keeping a small notebook after each session, jotting down his recurring symbols—the birds, the fire, the ocean, the glass. Over time, patterns began to emerge. When he spoke of birds, he meant thought and restlessness. Fire symbolized his racing mind. The ocean was his longing for calm, and broken glass appeared whenever he talked about relationships. His language wasn't random; it was systematic, structured by associations as consistent as any grammar. It became a map, intricate and delicate, guiding me through a mind shaped by experience, injury, and resilience.

I realized then that the key to helping him wasn't to pull him out of that language, but to learn it—to become fluent enough to translate its meanings back into something the world could understand. The more I understood, the more he trusted me with nuance. He began testing me, intentionally bending his metaphors to see if I could follow. Sometimes he'd smirk after saying something obscure, waiting to see if I could catch it. When I did, his entire demeanor softened, as if the weight of being misunderstood had momentarily lifted.

In those moments, I became his Rosetta Stone—the bridge between his inner world and the language of the outside world. Through reflection and translation, we began building a shared dictionary and slowly reintroduced him to direct expression. I would take one of his metaphors and gently mirror it back in plain speech, linking the two forms. If he said, "The fire's getting louder," I might respond, "So your thoughts feel restless again?" Over time, he began doing this independently, translating his own words as if he had come to realize the value of clarity. The metaphors didn't vanish; they evolved—becoming tools for connection rather than barriers to it.

The process was slow and delicate. There were days when progress seemed invisible—when our conversations spiraled into abstraction, and neither of us could quite find the thread. But there were also moments of revelation, when his metaphors began to dissolve into something simpler, more grounded. One afternoon, he paused mid-sentence and said, almost shyly, "I think what I meant is that I'm scared of losing control." It was the first time he had bridged the metaphor himself, translating the image before I could. That small act—those few words—carried more weight than any breakthrough I could have planned.

By the third or fourth month, a shift was noticeable. His stories were still rich with imagery, but the metaphors no longer dominated the conversation. They appeared like color rather than camouflage—adding depth rather than distortion. He began to speak more plainly about his emotions, his relationships, his fears. He no longer needed to cloak every thought in poetry to make it bearable. The more he trusted his words, the more he trusted himself. It was as if the language itself had become a mirror, reflecting both his inner world and his growing agency.

In learning his language, I hadn't just found a way to understand him—I had given him the means to understand himself. The metaphors had once been armor, then a bridge, and now they were becoming windows. What began as a puzzle of translation had turned into a process of reintegration, of reclaiming his voice piece by piece. Riley was starting to speak not just in symbols, but in truths—unfiltered, direct, and human. Each plain-spoken sentence felt like a small victory, proof that his mind and heart were aligning again.

By the time several more months had passed, a steady rhythm had taken hold. Riley's speech had shifted in a way that was both subtle and profound. The once-constant flow of metaphor had quieted, replaced by a clarity that felt deliberate, earned. He still used imagery, but now it served the message rather than obscuring it. His words carried intention—he chose them carefully, as if testing the strength of each before speaking it aloud. It was as though he was relearning how to live in a language that no longer needed to hide him.

Alongside this change came other markers of stability. Riley had stayed steady in his recovery for many months, something that had once felt impossible to him. The same mind that once sought refuge in old habits now sought it in purpose. He began talking about returning to school—something he'd left behind years earlier after the injury. He said he wanted to study something that "kept the gears moving," perhaps psychology or art, unsure which, but certain he wanted to learn again. There was an excitement in his voice when he spoke about it, a kind of hope that felt both unstable and real.

He also began to talk about the people close to him—family he had grown distant from over the years. At first, just in fragments—memories that still carried ache when he spoke of them. Over time, those fragments became plans.

He wanted to learn how to talk to them again, to explain himself without the storms of confusion that had once taken over every conversation. We spent sessions exploring what healthy communication might look like—how to pause before reacting, and how to listen without translating every emotion into metaphor. It wasn't easy for him, but the effort was sincere. His desire for reconnection had become his new compass.

I found myself encouraged by his progress, yet quietly wary. Change, especially linguistic and emotional change, is delicate—easily undone by stress, fatigue, or fear. There were moments when I'd hear the faint echo of his old speech patterns returning, a sudden shift into symbolism when a topic struck too close to the heart. Each time, my chest would tighten with concern, wondering if we were slipping backward into the abstract terrain we had worked so hard to navigate out of. But Riley now recognized the pattern himself. When it happened, he would stop, take a breath, and say, "That's the storm talking again." And then he'd rephrase, choosing clarity over comfort.

Those small moments of self-correction felt like victories. They showed not just awareness, but ownership—an understanding that his metaphors were no longer the only way to make sense of his world. He was beginning to master the balance between expression and connection, between the poetry of his inner life and the language that allowed others to meet him there. It was still a delicate balance, one that required vigilance and compassion, but it was progress built on genuine transformation.

As his counselor, I felt both pride and protectiveness. I knew how easily an old injury could reclaim its old vocabulary, how grief and frustration could tempt a return to the safety of metaphor. Still, I had come to believe that Riley no longer lived entirely within that language—he had learned how to step outside it when needed, to translate himself when the moment required it. He was no longer just surviving the chaos of his mind; he was learning how to narrate his way out of it.

Over the subsequent few sessions, Riley and I began translating his abstract progress into something concrete—a treatment plan he could see, measure, and take pride in. We turned his ideas into clear, realistic goals. Together, we laid out the foundation of a plan that aligned with his recovery and his desire to reconnect with the world beyond his metaphors. The plan became a tangible reflection of his emerging self-mastery.

The first goal focused on school. Riley had often spoken of wanting to "rebuild the bridge that burned behind me," which I came to understand meant reclaiming the part of himself that valued learning. We broke this down into manageable steps: contacting programs, meeting with advisors, completing applications, and setting a realistic timeline for starting classes. Each step was written out—something tangible to hold himself accountable to.

A second goal focused on rebuilding communication with the people close to him. We reframed this as a process of trial and error—learning through experience how to express himself more clearly, more directly, and without the heavy use of metaphor that had once created distance. He began practicing short, honest statements, testing how they landed, and reflecting afterward on what worked and what didn't. Each attempt became a small experiment in vulnerability and honesty.

The final goal addressed his ongoing recovery and stability. He would keep showing up to sessions, stay connected to whatever support kept him grounded, and check in regularly to notice what was working and where the metaphors might be creeping back in.

As we finalized the plan, I felt a cautious optimism. The old Riley had used language to obscure and deflect, but this version was beginning to use it to build structure. Still, I couldn't ignore my concern that his metaphors—his armor—might resurface if life pressed too hard again. So, while we signed the treatment plan together, I silently reminded myself that progress with Riley would always require translation.

Over the following months, the progress was unmistakable. Riley began to speak with a new steadiness, choosing clarity over metaphor in moments where, before, abstraction had dominated. He became noticeably more patient—with himself, with others, and with the slow rhythms of daily life. Conversations that once spiraled into confusion now landed with intention, and the subtle self-corrections he had begun early on became automatic. His relationships with the people close to him improved. Simple gestures—direct statements, listening without deflection, showing up consistently—began to rebuild trust and closeness.

School became a new arena for growth. Riley embraced the structure and accountability it provided, completing assignments on time, participating in group projects, and engaging with classmates in ways that reflected his developing ability to communicate clearly and collaborate effectively. The sense of accomplishment he gained there reinforced his self-confidence, proving that he could thrive in environments that had once felt overwhelming. Each milestone—finishing a paper, contributing to a discussion, meeting a deadline—was a reminder that the mind, even when reshaped by old injury, could adapt and excel with patience, guidance, and persistence.

Over time, his consistent efforts created a new rhythm in his life. Recovery was maintained, school attendance was regular, and communication with those he cared about continued to improve. Riley's metaphors had not disappeared, but they had transformed into tools he could wield intentionally—artful flourishes rather than barriers to understanding. He had become fluent not only in his own symbolic language but in the ordinary language of connection, patience, and trust.

By the time our work together reached its conclusion—after many months of steady effort—both of us had developed confidence in his future. Riley had learned to navigate the terrain of his mind, translating what once was opaque into meaning, action, and connection. Our sessions, once filled with riddles and abstraction, had become opportunities for clarity and insight. The bridges we had built together—between metaphor and reality, isolation and connection, survival and thriving—felt strong and enduring. It was a quiet triumph of patience, presence, and the slow art of understanding.

When our final session came, there was no grand proclamation, no dramatic closure. Instead, there was a mutual acknowledgment of achievement. Riley had discovered the tools to continue his journey, and I had witnessed the resilience and ingenuity of a mind that refused to be defined by its old injury. We reflected on the work that had been done, then parted with the confidence that he would continue to thrive, carrying forward the lessons of language, patience, and self-awareness that had become the foundation of his transformation.

In the end, Riley's journey was a testament to the power of language—not just words, but the bridges we build between thought and expression, metaphor and meaning, isolation and connection. Through patience, trust, and translation, he had learned to navigate the landscapes of his mind, turning storms into maps and fragments into coherence. His recovery was not just about staying steady or gaining skill but about reclaiming a voice that could speak both in poetry and in clarity, a voice that would carry him forward long after our work together had ended.

Riley's story remains a reminder that healing is a dialogue between mind, heart, and language, and that even the most abstract journeys can lead to tangible growth.

ABOUT THE AUTHOR

J. Alexander is a licensed therapist, addiction counselor, and clinical supervisor with over a decade of experience guiding individuals and families through the labyrinths of trauma, recovery, and relational healing. Holding a Master's in Counseling Psychology and a CADC III credential, he has worn many hats in the field—from case manager and residential treatment counselor to Intensive Outpatient Program coordinator and lead supervisor in high-stakes treatment environments. His career began in the trenches of residential addiction programs, where the raw pulse of human struggle first reshaped his understanding of resilience, and evolved into a private practice devoted to couples therapy, trauma-informed care, and the subtle art of bearing witness. Drawing from sessions that have etched themselves into his soul, Alexander's writing in Tales From the Chair transforms composite stories of the "hurt, the haunted, and the healed" into a testament to empathy's quiet power. A devoted husband and father of three whose own "growing pains" inform his compassionate lens, he resides in California, where he continues to step into the chair—not just to listen, but to remind us all that healing is a shared, stubborn miracle.

www.ingramcontent.com/pod-product-compliance
Lightning Source LLC
LaVergne TN
LVHW051423080426
835508LV00022B/3220